THE TEA CEREMONY

THE TEA CEREMONY

Sen'ō Tanaka

Foreword by EDWIN O. REISCHAUER

Preface by YASUSHI INOUE

Photography by TAKESHI NISHIKAWA

H·A·R·M·O·N·Y B·O·O·K·S

NEW YORK, NEW YORK

Acknowledgments

The author and photographer wish to thank the following art gallery and museums for their cooperation in granting permission to reproduce here some of the items in their collection—the Suntory Art Gallery: p. 31; the Fujita Art Museum: p. 28, 30, 34; the Gotō Art Museum: p. 29, 32, 35, 39 and p. 37 (scroll and celadon vase), 38 (tea caddy, tray, water jar and bowl), 40 (scroll), 41 (bowl, scoop, water jar and kettle).

Published by Kodansha International Ltd., 2–12–21 Otowa, Bunkyo-ku, Tokyo 112, Japan and Kodansha International/USA, Ltd., 10 East 53rd Street, New York 10022 and 44 Montgomery Street, San Francisco, California 94104. Copyright © 1973 by Kodansha International Ltd.

Harmony Books
A division of Crown Publishers, Inc.
One Park Avenue
New York, New York 10016

Published simultaneously in Canada by General Publishing Company Limited.

Printed in Japan.

Library of Congress Cataloging in Publication Data

Tanaka, Sen'ō, 1928–
    The tea ceremony.

    Includes index.
    1. Japanese tea ceremony. I. Title.
GT2910.T2978   1977   ˙394.1'2   77–1260
ISBN 0–517–530392

CONTENTS

FOREWORD

For the foreigner, it is hard to bring Japan into focus. Is the real Japan to be found in mammoth tankers, soaring production figures and seething mobs of commuters, or does it still reside in cherry blossoms, geisha, and Mt. Fuji? Is it the fleeting glimpse from the window of the "bullet train" of a thatched cottage in a neatly tailored, verdant valley surrounded by gently bending bamboo, or is it the train itself—that epitome of late twentieth-century technology and social engineering? Is it the fanatic soldiers of the Imperial Army of a generation ago or the equally determined young Japanese of today, locked in desperate combat with a brutal examination system, demonstrating violently in the streets on behalf of world peace, or circling the globe with earnest intent to discover the whole world and imbibe its essence? Is it the serenity of medieval gardens and Buddhist sculpture or the pollution and traffic jams of Tokyo and Osaka? Is it the inner calm of Zen philosophy or the red tape and frustrations of modern urban life? Japan is, of course, none of these, but it is all of them and a great deal more.

It is unreasonable to think that all the rich diversity of Japan can be brought into a single sharp focus. How could we do this for our own countries? I cringe when I hear Japanese attempting to interpret the vast complexities of the United States by some single touchstone—be it the Puritan spirit, Thoreau, Lincoln, the frontier spirit, capitalism, Vietnam or whatever. The rich culture of the British Isles cannot be reduced to one single equation, much less that of Japan, which today and throughout recorded history has had twice or more the population of the British Isles.

Still, some aspects of a civilization do stand out as being especially revealing of the best in that culture. They hint at, even if they do not fully define, those underlying strata of the psyche that give a culture its flavor and distinctiveness. The tea ceremony is certainly one of these features for Japan. It cannot bring all of Japanese civilization into focus, but it does offer a window that looks deeply into the Japanese soul.

Unfortunately the tea ceremony is not a window that is easily opened. It has often proved as mystifying to foreigners as informative. In a nation that loves tradition, the tea ceremony over the centuries has become so heavily encrusted with the barnacles of tradition that it has all but lost forward motion as a means of artistic expression. Transformed in modern mass society into a polite accomplishment for all girls of breeding, it has become a homogenized mass product. Enshrined as part of the mystique of a unique Japanese culture, it is casually sampled, along with seaweed or raw fish, by hordes of twittering foreigners. I can remember seeing rows of disinterested tourists gulping down their allotted tea before rushing on to the next "experience," while loudspeakers blared forth about the spirituality of the tea ceremony. I can remember one particularly grotesque episode, when a couple of dozen news photographers smashed down the surrounding sliding doors in their eagerness to take flashbulb shots of Mr. and Mrs. Robert Kennedy accompanied by my wife and me, attempting to look as though we were enjoying a quiet aesthetic moment.

Despite all this mistreatment, however, the tea ceremony does run deep and strong and pure. I am no specialist on the subject, but I have had enough intimate experience with it to be sure that this statement is true. In my days as a graduate student in Kyoto, my wife took flower arrangement lessons from a lady teacher who also taught the tea ceremony. Over a period of several months, I joined her once a week at her teacher's home to participate in tea ceremony sessions. Neither of us studied how to make or serve the tea, but we did learn how to play our role as participants in what became increasingly a deeply felt aesthetic and spiritual experience. In a sense we moved into a different world in time and space. There was no schedule. Everything moved at a slow pace quite detached from the rest of our lives. Our attention focused down to just a few objects of beauty, again quite removed from the world of overflowing abundance outside. There was a sense of sinking deep within one's own self, of being at harmony with nature, of finding all in very little.

I find it hard to describe the experience, but I know that it has given me an understanding of aspects of Japanese culture that I otherwise would never have had. There really is something very important to be seen through the window of the tea ceremony, if one can but brush aside the encrustations of long tradition and the flim-flam of tourism and mass society. Many Japanese have attempted to help us peer through this window. *The Book of Tea* of the great art critic and thinker, Okakura Kakuzo (usually called Tenshin by the Japanese), was the first important effort more than two generations ago. Now Sen'ō Tanaka, a leading authority on the tea ceremony, offers his masterful guidance in this magnificent book. The tea ceremony is no "open sesame" for all of Japanese civilization, but it does offer a way to learn something about the innermost qualities of the Japanese and the riches they have to offer the world.

Belmont, Mass.,   EDWIN O. REISCHAUER
July 1973

PREFACE

It would perhaps be superfluous to repeat once again what an important role *chadō* played in the molding and shaping of Japanese culture. The tea ceremony, together with its basic aesthetic concepts of *wabi* and *sabi*, is one of the traditional arts of which we today are proud inheritors. *Chadō* has influenced our outlook on life, it has colored our beliefs and attitudes as well as the standards that so rigidly govern the Japanese people. Even the youth of today, although they have no interest in the tea ceremony, find it difficult to detach themselves from these strong traditional values that will remain with them all their lives.

Just as "Rome was not built in a day," the tea ceremony, too, was not developed in a short space of time. Its roots and origins are intricately interwoven with the historical development of Japan, and in order to understand the deeper, more spiritual aspects of its philosophy, it is imperative to refer to its long history, starting with the introduction of tea to Japan, the changes in the custom of tea-drinking during the Heian and Kamakura periods, and culminating in the lives of the great masters of tea who advanced the art. Men like Shukō and Jō-ō were the first to adopt Japanese terms and expressions in the art of the tea ceremony, and Rikyū, the most famous of them with his disciples Sōtan, Oribe, Enshū, Sekishū and Fumai, did much to illuminate the dark avenues of culture in their time.

It is almost impossible for one to write about the tea ceremony without complete immersion in the mainstream of Japanese cultural history. Furthermore it is difficult, even for a Japanese, to relate the art of the tea ceremony which constitutes so much philosophic thought, without meandering from the spiritual stream of its concept; yet, Sen'ō Tanaka has succeeded admirably.

He has concentrated all his efforts on preserving what is most valuable in *chadō*, and as president of the Dai Nippon Chadō Gakkai and a young master of the tea ceremony in Japan, he has done much to promote its popularity in this country. It has always been my belief that a history of *chadō* can only be written by a master who has dedicated his whole life to the tea ceremony. This book could not have been produced had Mr. Tanaka been only a scholar of the art, for it requires more than an academic treatise to conjure up, in everyday language, the spirit that lies within the walls of the tea room.

When the custom of drinking tea was first introduced to Japan, it was only too natural for its devotees to want to design a special room for this purpose. I say only too natural here, but there is no other country in the world, apart from Japan, where such tea rooms exist, and, therefore, this expression is really only applicable to the Japanese people. Thus, the foundation of *chadō* was laid when the first tea room came into existence, and its essence was present within this room even though it took centuries for the art to evolve into its present form.

With the establishment of tea rooms, special rules of etiquette which suited the atmosphere were inevitably created, and special utensils which preserved and enhanced this decorum were selected by tea masters who dedicated their whole lives toward perfecting the ceremony. Thus, the tea room served as a salon where men could come to enjoy peace of mind and purity of spirit, and at the same time appreciate art at a very refined and sophisticated level. The tea room also became a refuge where the hustle and bustle of daily life could be forgotten, replaced by a discipline of mind and body.

Yet what is truly amazing is that nothing special or extraordinary takes place. The host and guests simply engage in the act of making and drinking tea. But it is this act which is important, for in the smallness of the tea room, the whole universe—heaven, earth and life itself—can be evoked, or, as in the case of Rikyū, death confronted.

Mr. Tanaka is one of the very few tea masters born in the Shōwa period (1926—), and by writing this book he has added another leaf to the pages of the tea ceremony. He follows the path of the earlier great masters of tea who wrote of the ceremony in their lifetime. This, I believe, is the responsibility of all great tea masters throughout history, and I have great hopes in Mr. Tanaka's dedication.

This book, written with the Westerner in mind, follows *The Book of Tea* by Okakura Kakuzo (Tenshin), who published his classic in English in 1906. It is my heartfelt desire that this volume will, as Tenshin's did, enhance an understanding of Japanese culture. And, in conclusion, I would like to wish Mr. Tanaka great success in his noble pursuit.

Tokyo,   YASUSHI INOUE
July 1973

AUTHOR'S PREFACE

In a world atlas, the four main islands of Japan are curved in the shape of a crescent and situated in the temperate zone of the northern hemisphere, the same latitudinal sector as the East Coast of America. In spring the earth is awakened by the gentle call of rain, which bathes the trees and plants with their first foliage and breathes life into the slumbering fields. Summer is not a kind season, and the fiery heat of the sun drives most of us to the hills or the seaside. But soon autumn arrives and, with its southern winds and crisp cool air, turns the leaves to glowing hues of burnt orange and scorched yellow. When leaves fall from the trees and frost coats the ground, chilly winds from the north herald the approach of winter, which covers the earth with the white blanket of sleep.

The changes of season are received with both joy and sadness by the people, whose sentiments are conveyed in their greetings to each other. The seasons are also responsible for inspiring art and literature, for, according to the Russian writer Chekhov, creativity is firmly linked to climatic conditions. In an ideal climate, the feelings of the people are numbed by the pleasurable weather, while in places where the air is either bitterly cold or unbearably hot, there is little time left for thought after the struggle against natural odds. But in Japan, the seasons keep us constantly aware of the presence of nature and her many faces, an awareness to which the famous poet Bashō accredited the creation of typically Japanese arts.

My own gratitude to the four seasons increases as the years go by. I entered the Way of Tea as a child, and by the time I was a young man I knew that I would remain with it for life. My relationship with the seasons has always been very close, since perhaps in no other art does nature play such an important role, influencing all its aesthetics. We always decorate our tea rooms and use tea articles which are in harmony with the seasons, as though the tea ceremony itself had been created specially to sing the praises of the passing seasons.

In the pictures on pages 17–20, the photographer Takeshi Nishikawa and I have attempted to express what the Japanese feel about nature, perhaps in a more coherent way than words can. The picture of the cherry tree in early spring was selected to invoke the inherent beauty of the cherry blossoms.

The secret of moss lies in its soft, velvety depth. In Japan we use moss to decorate our gardens, even though moss does not grow easily in this country. I know the difficulty of cultivating these tiny plants, and I know the patience and tolerance required on the part of the cultivators. Yet I always feel a joyous beating in my heart on seeing the greenness of moss glistening in the rain, and I feel as though my heart and soul have been washed clean, like the moss.

The plate on page 19 captures the transient nature of autumn, the brief moment between scarlet splendor and bleak solitude. The term "burning leaves" is used to describe the transition of the leaves from an autumnal red to a golden yellow, for neither can survive the onset of winter.

Snow in the countryside—such is the serenity and severity of a Japanese winter. The picture on page 20 invokes the hushed atmosphere of snow covering the trees and valleys with a silvery glow.

Similar scenes are frequently echoed by the subtle ink paintings that hang in the alcove of the tea room. Such pictures of nature's magnificence are seemingly unaffected by the progress of civilization. To me the best expression of this perpetual rhythm of nature is the art of the tea ceremony, which, like nature, is timeless and untouched by the modernization of living. Nature and the tea ceremony have permeated our daily life, our manners, and indeed, our very souls.

Tokyo,   SEN'Ō TANAKA
July 1973

14

THE TEA CEREMONY

1. Spring at Arashiyama, Kyoto.

2. Summer at Saihō-ji, Kyoto.

3. Fall in the Imperial Palace of Kyoto.

4. Winter at Arashiyama, Kyoto.

CHA-NO-YU

Cha-no-yu, which literally means "hot water for tea," is known in English as the tea ceremony and has as its objective a relaxed communion between the host and his guests. It is based in part on the etiquette of serving tea, but it also includes the aesthetic contemplation of landscape gardens, tea utensils, paintings, flower arrangement, and all the other elements that coexist in a harmonious relationship with the ceremony. Its ultimate aim is the attainment of a deep spiritual satisfaction through the drinking of tea and through silent contemplation.

It is a uniquely composite form of art, created through the refinement of the Chinese custom of drinking tea, and distilled with elements of Zen philosophy, which gave it various symbols and rituals. On a different level, the tea ceremony is simply an entertainment where the guests are invited to drink tea in a pleasant and relaxing room. The bonds of friendship between the host and guests are strengthened in the ceremony when the host himself makes and serves the tea.

Each tea ceremony is supposed to be a unique experience, with its own particular mood that can never be duplicated. An expression was coined by the well-known master of the fifteenth century, Takeno Jō-ō, who performed each tea ceremony reverently because he believed it was "the one chance in one's lifetime." His famous pupil, Rikyū, took the lesson to heart when he shaved off all his hair for one of his master's ceremonies, as a mark of respect for the occasion.

The tea ceremony borrowed much from Zen religion because the first tea masters were priests, who, since the fourteenth century, had exerted a marked influence on Japanese culture and social customs. They taught their followers that enlightenment can only be reached through Zen meditation, and the tea ceremony became a means of disciplining the mind. Thus the saying originated that "tea and Zen are inseparable."

In the sixteenth century, when the art was handed down to the general population, the tea ceremony enjoyed widespread favor. Everyone, from nobles to commoners, found in it the ideal means of relaxation from the cares of the outside world; the tea room was a place where they could mix freely with anyone and yet cultivate their sense of appreciation of the forms of beauty in the setting and the use of special tea articles.

At the same time the spiritual aspect of the ceremony gave way, regrettably, to formal etiquette, as a special code of ethics was devised to govern the education of its devotees. This affected the general character of the tea cult, whose finer principles of inward spirituality were substituted by an increased concentration on outward form.

Thus, today, even the Japanese themselves retain this basic misconception of the depth of the tea ceremony, which is often regarded as a suitable accomplishment for young women before marriage. In the past fifty years, estimates show that ninety percent of students of the tea ceremony have been women, an unfortunate indication of the abuse of this unique form of art.

Cha-no-yu is a specialist form of art that calls for a good knowledge of architecture, landscape gardens, tea utensils, as well as the capacity to appreciate the total effect of their beauty. Thus it seems that etiquette, spirituality *and* knowledge are all necessary elements for the understanding of the tea ceremony. In the large tea gatherings of today, it is difficult to convey all these refined qualities, for the art of the tea ceremony is, by its very essence, founded on intimacy, spontaneity and subtlety.

EARLY HISTORY OF TEA

Reliance on China

Tea did not grow in Japan until the first seeds were brought from China during the T'ang dynasty (618–905), when cultural interchange between the two countries reached a peak. The first mention of a formal ceremony involving the drinking of tea is in the eighth century, when Emperor Shōmu (724–49) invited the monks who had participated in his religious service to take tea in his palace.[1]

At about the same time in China (760), a Buddhist priest by the name of Lu Wu completed the first book on tea called *Cha Ching*, which outlined all the rules for the correct method of making tea, such as the temperature of hot water and the proper use of tea vessels. It was largely through the influence of this classic that the form and style of today's tea ceremony evolved in Japan.

During the Nara period (710–84) tea plants were grown on the grounds of some temples and served priests and noblemen as a medicinal beverage. As tea was not imported in large quantities from China and was not grown extensively in Japan, it came to be regarded as a luxury commodity beyond the reach of the general populace. Its general appeal was further restricted when relations between the two countries deteriorated toward the end of the T'ang dynasty, and the Chinese development of tea from medicine to beverage did not spread to Japan until much later on. At the same time, Japan, which had previously imitated the more sophisticated culture of China, was forced to mold its own traditions and foster its own culture.

One outcome of this new development can be seen in the way Buddhism in Japan took on a different approach from Chinese Buddhism and crystallized into a purely Japanese religion. Similarly, the nobility began to create new pastimes based on a quest for aesthetics in the fields of art and calligraphy. As no records were kept of the Chinese custom of tea-drinking, the beverage remained virtually unknown from the Nara period until the Heian period (794–1192), but tea was re-introduced in different parts of Japan toward the end of the latter era and at the beginning of the Kamakura period (1192–1333).

It is almost certain that if tea had been grown in Japan, or was more readily available, the Japanese tea ceremony might not have been created, since its rules and formalities are based on the concept of tea as a rare and valuable commodity.

Introduction of Powdered Tea to Japan

The Kamakura period in Japanese history coincided to a large extent with the Southern Sung dynasty (1126–1278) of China, an epoch characterized by a high level of culture both in the fine and applied arts. A new systematic approach to learning in the fields of philosophy and religion attracted a number of Japanese priests and scholars to study in China. One of these priests, who left for China in 1187, was Eisai Myō-an, founder of Zen Buddhism in Japan. He returned to Japan in 1191 and planted the tea seeds he had brought with him in the Hizen district, later transplanting them to Hakata, Kyushu, where the first temple of his Rinzai sect[2] was built.

Eisai was the first to grow tea for a purely religious purpose; others before him had cultivated tea for medicinal use only. It was at this time that tea was becoming associated with the newly formulated canons of Zen, and the word *sarei*, meaning the etiquette of tea-making, was often applied in a religious connection.

The tea that Eisai grew was a great improvement in quality on the earlier types of tea grown in the country. This may have encouraged him to experiment with better ways for drinking it, which led to the discovery of powdered tea. Until then, people had boiled tea leaves in water, but Eisai taught them to grind the leaves

24

into powder, add hot water, and stir the mixture well before drinking it, which improved its flavor.

Powdered tea was first mentioned in a book by Tsan Hsiang, a noted Chinese calligrapher who worked under the Sung emperor Ren Tsung (1023–64). His book called *Cha Lu*, written in 1053, referred to the manufacture of powdered tea, the green tea which was incorporated into the tea ceremony in Japan. Another Sung emperor, Hui Tsung, referred to the bamboo whisk used to whip the tea after water was poured over it in his book called *Ta Kuan Cha Lun* or *A General View of Tea*. These were the first two imports from China which formed the basis of the modern tea ceremony in Japan.

Eisai aroused a great deal of hostility among the monks who disliked the new religion he had imported, but he succeeded in enlisting the protection of the Kamakura shogunate, whose members were among his earliest converts. In January 1211 he wrote the first treatise on tea in Japan, *Kissa Yōjōki* or *Tea-drinking is Good for Health*, a small booklet of twenty pages in praise of tea, strongly recommending it as a cure for five types of disease: loss of appetite, drinking water disease, paralysis, boils and beri-beri. Tea, he added, is a remedy for all disorders, perhaps a reason for the consequent popularity of tea-drinking.

The priests were also among the first to appreciate tea as a beverage, especially Myō-e of the Kōzan-ji temple in Togano-o, who was given some tea seeds by Eisai in 1207. Myō-e, who cultivated tea as an ascetic part of his religious life, produced excellent crops with these seeds in Fukase, and it is said that the tea produced there today comes from the plantations of Myō-e.

In 1221, when the power of the Kamakura shogun was more secure, Myō-e found a larger area in Uji district near Kyoto and transplanted his tea shrubs there in order to meet the growing demand for tea. The number of tea drinkers increased rapidly, especially among the upstart samurai. This warrior class, which was beginning to seek a legal basis of government to counteract the former aristocratic regime in Kyoto, turned eagerly to everything offered by the Sung dynasty: legal and political systems, religion and, naturally, tea. It is quite probable that, had the court nobles still been in power, there would have been little opportunity for the import of new knowledge from outside Japan.

Tea and the Samurai

After the fall of the Kamakura shogunate in 1333, Japan was thrown into a state of confusion by the rivalries between the Northern and Southern dynasties. During the civil wars a new class of people came into existence, *gekokujō* or the parvenus, whose extravagant lifestyle quickly attracted the attention of the public. Most of these upstart nobles were interested in tea-drinking for entertainment, and they often held large gatherings with their friends to enjoy tea and play *tōcha*,[3] a game that originated in the Sung dynasty of China. At first the game was not combined with drinking tea, but soon both activities merged into a single pastime.

The guests were tested on their ability to distinguish between the two types of tea grown in the country: genuine tea, or *honcha*, which designated the tea grown at Togano-o, and fake tea, *hicha*, for tea grown elsewhere. Later, however, as tea came to be grown in many places around the country, the game developed into a test of the players' knowledge of tea regions, plantations and names of specific kinds of tea. Betting soon accompanied these games, and the winners were presented with valuable ornaments, furniture, and even imported Chinese artifacts as prizes, which added to the excitement of the games.

Tōcha was played by people from all classes and was not confined to the nobility. There are frequent allusions to the games in the diaries of priests and nobles, and in the *Taiheiki*,[4] the famous chronicle of the civil war. It refers to one host of a *tōcha* gathering who offered one hundred different kinds of stakes, while another piled up one hundred rolls of dyed silk before the players, and a third provided ten different kimono as prizes. In this way the hosts could flaunt their own wealth as well as decorate their homes with precious works of art on these occasions. Such art displays also added to the enjoyment of the game.

The system of serving tea was extremely elaborate. There were originally ten cups of four different kinds of tea for each guest, but soon the number of cups increased to twenty, thirty, fifty and seventy, until it reached one hundred cups per person. A tea party in which fifty or sixty cups of tea were served in a ceremonial manner took a long time; therefore, a banquet including the serving of liquor was given, and tea was drunk between courses. It was not unusual for such a party to last from early morning until far into the night.

It is unknown in what order people drank the tea, but most probably it was done by passing the cup from one guest to the other. If there were a great number of people present it would have been impossible to serve tea in individual cups: for instance in a gathering of sixty-three people, if each guest drank 50 cups, it would have required 3,150 cups to entertain all of them. The technique of passing around one cup originated in these huge feasts, and probably explains why only one bowl is used in today's tea ceremony.

Another activity in which one object was shared among many participants was ceremonial incense-smelling, a popular recreation among court nobles. In this type of game the participants sampled four different kinds of incense, ten times each. The average number of guests was usually ten, and they would pass one incense burner among them. If more than one incense burner was used, the smell could vary according to the level of heat in the different burners.

This habit of sharing might seem odd today, but it stems from the samurai class which had strong family ties, and when they gathered on important occasions, it was the custom for the lord to take the first sip of sake from a large cup and pass it among his retainers, an indication of friendship and the close relationship among them.

Tea and the Ashikaga Family

When the civil wars came to an end in 1392, the parvenu nobles, who had accumulated both power and wealth, took control of the country with Ashikaga Takauji (1305–58) as the first Muromachi shogun. The Tenryū-ji temple at Saga, near Kyoto, was built by him in 1339 to commemorate the death of Emperor Godaigo, who had perished in the struggle between the Northern and Southern dynasties,[5] and the chief priest at Tenryū-ji was a certain Musō Kokushi (1275–1351), a leading Zen teacher and master of landscape gardening and architecture. This appointment opened the way for other Zen priests to play a more important role in worldly society, and the ensuing close harmonious relationship between religion and government had a profound influence on the tranquil and simple spirit that typified the Muromachi era.

During the rule of Ashikaga Takauji, the tea game was so popular that he had to issue a ban against it. At the same time, a new style of tea gathering was evolving, called *cha-e*, an older form of *cha-no-yu*, the formal tea ceremony of today. Nevertheless it was *tōcha* which enjoyed greater popularity among soldiers and common people, who also started to place small bets on tea guessing. The *Tōji Temple Chronicle* in Kyoto relates that in 1403, a shop in front of the temple was selling tea by the cup, an indication of the popularity of tea with the general public. Even priests and temple attendants of Kyoto indulged in the tea game. In another temple chronicle, *Kyōkaku Shiyōshū*, mention is made of a more ribald form of sport called the *rinkan* tea gathering, where taking a hot bath was combined with the pleasures of drinking tea.

In 1397, the third Ashikaga shogun, Yoshimitsu (1358–1408), built an elaborate palace at Kitayama, Kyoto, where he used to entertain his friends. The palace design combined elements of both Northern and Southern Sung styles, which was called *karayō*, or literally, Chinese style.

In the *Correspondence on Tea-drinking* (*Kissa Ōrai*), which was written during

Yoshimitsu's time, the order and ritual of a tea party were described in some detail. The guests, after enjoying the host's hospitality, left their banquet seats and went out to the garden, where there was an arbor for tea entertainment. The arbor was actually designed for moon-viewing, and a scaffold commanding a view in all directions was built on the roof of the pavilion. Hanging on the walls of the moon-viewing room were Chinese paintings and scrolls, and the guests relaxed with ten bowls each of four different kinds of tea. It seems likely that the Kinkaku-ji (Golden Pavilion) in Kyoto was used as a tea arbor in earlier days.

It was the custom in those days to decorate homes and moon-viewing arbors with Chinese art, since the Kamakura culture was strongly under the influence of the Sung and Yuan dynasties. The priests who traveled between China and Japan frequently brought back important works of art with them, which they later displayed in their temples. The influence was to spread even further during the Muromachi period when trade was intensified between Japan and Ming-dynasty China. In a record of the Enkaku-ji temple of Kamakura written in 1363 (*Butsunichi-an Kōbutsu Mokuroku*), there is a list of its Chinese possessions which include twenty paintings by the famous Zen painters Mu Ch'i[6] and Li Ti. In addition, the *Imperial Lists of Treasures and Paintings* also mention a great number of Chinese art objects that formed part of Japanese collections.

Japanese architecture of the Muromachi period was transformed from the formal palace style of the Heian period to a simplified samurai style, and then into the *shoin* style, which incorporated elements of temple architecture. *Shoin* details were adopted for the design of tea ceremony rooms: the alcove (*tokonoma*), for instance, developed from the decorative platform set in front of the Buddhist scroll in a noble's bedchamber, the pair of shelves (*chigaidana*) in the side of the alcove was formerly used to display precious ornaments, while the side alcove (*tsuke-shoin*) served as a desk. Finally the floor of these rooms was also covered with straw tatami mats, in the *shoin* style.

Originally, the *shoin* room served as a study/drawing room, where visitors could also be entertained with tea. Near the drawing room was a shelf called *taji*, equipped with the necessary tea articles such as a charcoal brazier and a kettle, which enabled the host to make tea in the drawing room and carry it to his guests. The *taji* had also formerly been a part of temple design, and in the Muromachi period was incorporated into the interior of houses.

Gradually, the way of decorating the alcove, the shelves in the side alcove, and the *shoin* desk began to have a fixed form, with the aim of arranging a small number of articles aesthetically and functionally. This became a hobby of the samurai nobles, but was still inaccessible to the general public.

After some time, tea came to be served ceremonially in the *shoin* by menservants attired as monks, who were known as *dōbōshū*. The articles used for tea during this period were all imported from China: charcoal brazier, water jar, ladle stand, and lid rest. All these were arranged in the tea cabinet, and the ceremony was performed by the *dōbōshū*.

A fine example of *shoin* architecture may be found in the Ginkaku-ji (Silver Pavilion), which Ashikaga Yoshimasa (1435–90) constructed as part of his villa in Higashiyama, Kyoto, in 1482. The Silver Pavilion, in contrast to the Golden Pavilion, is more sophisticated in appearance, with an atmosphere that conveys a sense of profundity in its simplicity.

The Founder of *Cha-no-yu*

The tea ceremony vogue among the aristocrats attracted the attention of other classes as well, who sought to imitate the etiquette of tea-making developed by the samurai nobles, even though they could not afford the same magnificent rooms and decorations. This did not deter them from holding similar gatherings in smaller, less lavish rooms that were appropriate to their social status.

The samurai also used smaller rooms when they entertained only a few of their guests, since a small room was not only more comfortable but also less formal. These small rooms were actually the corners of large rooms partitioned off by a screen, or *kakoi*, and later on, when smaller rooms were built specially for this purpose, they became known as *kakoi*.

One of the best designers of smaller tea rooms was a Zen priest by the name of Murata Shukō (1422–1502), known as the father of the tea ceremony, for the spirit and etiquette of tea were originated by him. His actual existence has been in doubt, but new data has been found which throws some light on his life.

Shukō was born in Nara and entered the priesthood at Shōmyō-ji temple at the age of eleven. When he was twenty he left the temple, only to return again ten years later to enter the priesthood. He studied Zen meditation under the monk and teacher Ikkyū Sōjun at Daitoku-ji temple in Kyoto. Shortly after he began his studies, he distinguished himself by his understanding of the religion, and was presented with a diploma signed by the Chinese sage Yuan Wu. It is said that he hung the scroll of writing on the wall of his tea room in Nara and spent the rest of his days perfecting the tea ceremony as well as giving lessons to those who were interested in learning the art.

Shukō initiated one important procedure which differed from that of earlier tea masters, and that is, he would serve tea to his guests himself. Although it was more usual to hold large tea gatherings in a *shoin* room, Shukō preferred the intimate and personal atmosphere of a small room where five or six people could communicate through the medium of tea. This became a fundamental ruling for all future tea ceremonies. The four-and-a-half-mat tea room (9 sq. yds.) which he devised in order to create a more tranquil atmosphere for the performance of the ceremony had its origins in Zen philosophy, which Shukō studied at Kyoto. He particularly disliked the undignified, boisterous *rinkan* tea gatherings of Nara, where the enjoyment of tea was combined with the ritual of a bath.

In a letter to his favorite pupil Harima no Furuichi, Shukō outlined his own basic concept of the art of *cha-no-yu* and his personal outlook on aesthetics. He discussed the idea of refined simplicity, or *kareru*, at length, a theme which was much debated in his time, and he frowned upon the use of sophisticated, sober-colored pottery from Bizen and Shigaraki[7] by novices who had inadequate knowledge of their aesthetic qualities. His letter also reveals that Shukō took great pains to study the most aesthetic method of combining Japanese with Chinese tea utensils.

In the *Record of Yamanoue Sōji*, Shukō is referred to as *kaisan*, or the founder of the tea ceremony, which indicates that Shukō was already highly regarded in his time by other tea masters. Nō-ami,[8] for instance, the teacher of the shogun Ashikaga Yoshimasa, was only called *dōbōshū*, or one who established the rules of ceremonial tea-making in the *shoin* tea room. Mention is also made of Shukō's preference for the four-and-a-half-mat tea room.

The language followed the new spirit of the age, and a host of new words were coined which combined the practical details of life with aesthetics: *suki*, for instance, meaning a "liking of tea," came also to mean "artistic taste." It was only in the sixteenth century that the expression *cha-no-yu* was used to describe a tea gathering where the host himself served tea for a small party of friends.

When the tea culture reached a peak of popularity toward the end of the Muromachi period, tea devotees were given different titles to distinguish their relation to the art. *Cha-no-yu-sha* was the name given to a professional teacher of the tea ceremony like Shukō. A *wabi-suki* was a teacher distinguished by three particular qualities: faith in the performance of tea, an ability to act with decorum befitting a proper master, as well as excellent practical skills. Finally the *mei-jin* not only met all the qualifications of the *wabi-suki*, but was a collector of fine Chinese tea utensils as well.

FOOTNOTES

1. In the eighth century the Buddhist service included an event called *incha*, in which the emperor invited all the monks participating in the religious service to drink tea with him in the palace. It would seem that the custom of tea-drinking was adopted by the imperial family soon after it was introduced to Japan.

2. One sect of Zen Buddhism is named after the Chinese monk Lin Chi I Hsuan. In 1191, after four years in China, Eisai Myō-an brought home the Rinzai faith, which he spread first in Chikuzen, then in Kyoto and Kamakura. Eisai's branch has now been divided into ten secondary branches, which possess over 6,000 temples and close to two million believers.

3. This tea-guessing game was first introduced from China in the latter half of the Kamakura period where friends assembled to drink and enjoy tea as well as to distinguish the difference between tea grown in various provinces of Japan. Interest in *tōcha* persisted until the middle of the Muromachi period, and many lavish prizes were donated to the winners. In later days, the game became more refined, and came to be included in one variation of *temae* in the tea ceremony today.

4. The famous war chronicle in forty volumes which describes the battles between the Northern and Southern dynasties from 1333–92 is attributed to a priest called Kojima.

5. The two branches of the imperial family, which split into the Northern and Southern dynasties in 1333, fought over control of the country in a civil war that lasted fifty years.

6. A Zen monk and painter who lived during the late thirteenth century and is most famous for his "Eight Scenes of Hsiao Hsiang".

7. Bizen pottery produced from modern Okayama Prefecture is a fine-textured, red-bodied stoneware, originally produced for domestic use, but as tea masters turned to these wares after the fifteenth century, the kilns produced numerous tea utensils. Old Bizen is usually unglazed, except for occasional accidental spots or smears of gloss. Shigaraki ware was produced since the Kamakura period in Shiga Prefecture and, compared to Bizen ware, is thicker in texture.

8. Nō-ami (1397–1471) was a painter and poet and served the Ashikaga household as the *dōbōshū*, in charge of the evaluation of Chinese art. He is also the author of *Kundaikan Sōchōki*, a catalog of works in the possession of the Ashikaga family, which is invaluable today as a source of knowledge of the art of the day.

TEA MASTERS AND TEA STYLES

The Beginning of the Modern Age

The sixteenth century proved an exciting age for Japan with the influx of Portuguese traders in 1549, who not only brought with them a new religion but also opened new markets on its shores. This economic development brought about an expansion of the middle class: the wealthy merchants who had profited by trading with the Europeans gained a certain amount of respectability, hitherto only reserved for the nobility, as a result of their achievements. The same spirit of adventure characterized their ruler, a former daimyo, Oda Nobunaga (1534–82),[1] who opposed the traditional authority of the court nobles and wrested power from their hands during the civil wars which were to last until 1600. He governed the country along more democratic lines than did his predecessors, and this spirit of democracy was to leave a strong impression on the ritual of tea.

Japanese architecture also developed along more inventive and more independent lines during his rule. While the Asuka period (592–710) had imitated Sui and T'ang styles, and the Kamakura period had depended on the Sung dynasty for new ideas, architecture during Nobunaga's era concentrated on distinctly Japanese designs for the construction of castles, homes and tea houses. This marks a break with the older tradition of imitating temple designs for the construction of residential houses.

Perhaps it was a sign of the troubled times that the samurai warriors, acutely aware of the shadow of death following them from one war to the next, sought refuge from the grimness of life in the tea room. There, secure from the cares of the world, they were able to retreat peacefully into a spiritual universe. Perhaps too, for the same reason, they preferred to build and decorate their castles in a more flamboyant and colorful style than their predecessors. They did not hesitate to incorporate European designs in their homes, from architecture to furniture to clothes, all of which were readily copied by the merchants.

The Tea Ceremony Is Introduced to Sakai

Today the city of Sakai is one of several small towns in the commercial and industrial complex of Osaka Prefecture, but in the two hundred years between the Muromachi and Momoyama ages, Sakai developed from a small fishing village into a prosperous commercial port. Trade with China was reestablished in the fifteenth century, with Sakai as the entrepôt between the two countries, and with the steady influx of merchants who came to trade in Sakai, it quickly became the most active business center of Japan.

The inhabitants of Sakai benefited financially under these conditions since the city was not in the possession of feudal lords but directly under the control of the government. Its inhabitants were people of all classes, including priests, court nobles and warriors, and they were usually referred to as the *machi-shū*,[2] or those living in a self-governing town.

The administration of the city was carried out in fairly democratic terms by the *egō-shū*, or townsmen who met to formulate new laws. These men took pains not to tread on the toes of the powerful lords, and many meetings were convened to promote friendly ties with them. So, when the tea ceremony spread to Sakai, it rapidly became the most popular form of entertainment, since it made socializing so much easier than the complicated *renga* competitions where people gathered to compose rhyming verse.

As a rule, these tea gatherings were held in private homes where anyone, whether he was acquainted with the host or not, could attend. It was rather like admiring works of art or eating a meal—anyone could casually join a group of people, regardless of his social status, at least until the more elaborate and rigid rules were devised which precluded certain classes of people from mixing freely with their social superiors.

There were two leaders of the tea cult in Sakai, Torii Insetsu, who did not have much effect in his time, and Takeno Jō-ō, who distinguished himself in his lifetime by enriching the forms and accessories of the art. Both men were students of Shukō, the earlier master, and Jō-ō was a *machi-shū*, well-versed in poetry as well as Zen Buddhism. He decided to enter the priesthood after fighting in the ten-year war of Ishiyama during which he had become extremely aware of the uncertainty of human life in the temporal world.

According to the *Record of Yamanoue Sōji*, Jō-ō had first practiced the tea ceremony according to the teachings of Shukō, but later on he improved on his master's techniques. Jō-ō's status as the leading master and innovator of his time was also enhanced by his large collection of over sixty different kinds of tea utensils, when most of his contemporaries could only boast a few. Jō-ō's influence as a tea connoisseur even spread to Kyoto, where devotees copied his style of tea rooms, his arrangement of tea articles, his method of preparing tea and the correct form of the ceremony.

In the historical accounts given of the end of the sixteenth century, there is evidence that the advances the inhabitants of Sakai were making in the tea ceremony were more profound and refined compared with those of the other major cities. The samurai nobles, for instance, were still serving elaborate banquet meals to accompany their tea ceremonies, while the *machi-shū* entertained their guests on a much simpler level. This did not mean that they were less wealthy, but the philosophy behind their concept of the tea ceremony and its purpose differed greatly from the more vulgar ostentatiousness of the samurai. This ideal of simplicity in the art of tea was emphasized by Jō-ō in his teachings to his pupils. His favorite motto was a poem of Fujiwara no Teika[3] which says:

Where are the crimson leaves,
Flowers of the season?
Only a little hut on the long curving bay
Stands in the serenity of an autumn evening.

This, for Jō-ō, expressed the very heart and essence of the tea ceremony.

Toyotomi Hideyoshi and the Tea Ceremony

The tea ceremony also came to be used as a means of courting favors from powerful men who lived during the troubled age of Oda Nobunaga. Nobunaga himself had made use of the ceremony to impress the wealthy merchants of Sakai who controlled the import of military weapons from Portugal.[4] For this purpose he invited the *machi-shū* to tea gatherings where he used tea utensils belonging to the Ashikaga clan, a diplomatic way of revealing that the authority of the Ashikagas was now vested in him. Frequently, as a reward to his generals, he would make gifts of these articles, which were highly prized because of their association with distinguished previous owners. Thus the tea ceremony came to be popular even among the hardened military men of those times.

The successor to Nobunaga, Toyotomi Hideyoshi,[5] was well known for his political genius, and his rise from the low rank of a samurai warrior to the ruler of the entire country is an indication of his military ability. When he heard of Nobunaga's death, he rushed back from the front and disposed of his chief rival, Akechi Mitsuhide,[6] in a fierce battle[7] that followed the struggle for power. When Hideyoshi assumed complete control over the country, he also indulged in political maneuvers to secure political alliances by way of the tea ceremony.

Hideyoshi held a large tea gathering a month after he defeated Mitsuhide in 1582, and two more in the six months that followed. The third one, to which the leading merchants of Kyoto and Sakai were invited, took place in Yamazaki. Like Nobunaga before him who made great show of using those utensils belonging to his predecessors to flaunt his power, Hideyoshi would display Nobunaga's collection whenever he entertained his generals. In the same way, he wished to indicate that he was the rightful successor to Nobunaga through the use of his tea articles, which had once belonged to the powerful Ashikaga clan. Hideyoshi also acquired the habit of publicly exhibiting the collection of articles he inherited, and this was done after Osaka Castle was constructed in 1590.

Hideyoshi conquered the entire country from Shikoku to Kyushu and was appointed regent in 1585. As a token of his gratitude to the emperor and princes, Hideyoshi himself served tea at a small house inside the Imperial Palace. This was the first time that a ceremony was performed at court with a daimyo doing the honors. Hideyoshi was so fond of the tea ceremony that he had a golden tea pavilion built that same year which could be carried away with him to Kyushu.[8]

In 1587 the "Great Tea Ceremony" was held at Kitano, Kyoto, where all classes of people were invited to attend, including priests and aristocrats. On that morning Hideyoshi acted as host, making tea for the 803 people who arrived for the ceremony. As this event was repeated on several other occasions, the popularity of *cha-no-yu* spread very rapidly.

One interesting question that comes to mind is whether Hideyoshi used the tea ceremony only as a means of furthering his political career. It is quite obvious that he entertained his political allies lavishly to display the valuable acquisitions he had inherited, but it is also true to say that he gradually found intense enjoyment in the art of *cha-no-yu* itself. It is written by chroniclers that Hideyoshi liked to meditate in a small hut when he was not entertaining on a grand scale.

In January 1584, Hideyoshi held a tea gathering inside the premises of what was later Osaka Castle, in a secluded tea room called the Yamazato. The ceremony itself was to commemorate the opening of this tea room which was specially built for him and named Yamazato, meaning a rural place. The tea room itself was only two tatami mats, or six feet square, and Hideyoshi often used it for more intimate meetings. A similar Yamazato room was also built inside Fushimi Castle which Hideyoshi constructed after he turned the position of regent over to his son Hidetsugu. There, Hideyoshi spent his last years in complete tranquillity and seclusion, showing a side of his character that was doubtlessly influenced by his teacher and master, Sen no Rikyū.[9]

Rulers and Tea Masters

It became customary for rulers to enlist the aid of their most trusted tea masters in times of stress. When the inhabitants of Sakai refused to contribute to the war expenditure incurred by Nobunaga, he sought the help of one of his three chief tea masters, called *sadō*,[10] to regain their support. Imai Sōkyū was thus able to prevent a rebellion in Sakai, whose people had hired samurai mercenaries to defend their stand. Tsuda Sōgyū, another *sadō* and head of the rich merchant class, cooperated with Sōkyū, and thus secured the friendship of Nobunaga, and was often invited to his castles at Gifu and Azuchi. The third *sadō* who was associated with Nobunaga was Sen no Rikyū.

Nobunaga held a tea gathering at Shōkoku-ji temple in Kyoto in 1574 at which the merchants of Sakai were also present. It was at this ceremony, where he displayed his prized incense burner which he named *chidori* (plover), that he presented two of his *sadō* with the sacred *Ranjatai* incense.[11] This gift to Sōgyū and Rikyū was an indication that he valued their friendship. Only Sōkyū, who was already held in great esteem by his ruler, was not presented with incense.

After Nobunaga's death at Honnō-ji temple, the three tea masters were forced to take sides between the contenders for his title, Mitsuhide and Hideyoshi. Both Sōkyū and Sōgyū sent messengers to the two rivals inquiring after their health, but Rikyū lost no time and rushed straight to Hideyoshi's side.

After his victory, Hideyoshi retained all three of Nobunaga's tea masters, largely through necessity, in order to consolidate his power and make use of their connections. According to the *Record of Yamanoue Sōji*, Hideyoshi had eight masters working for him, although his biography reveals that he employed Sōkyū, Sōgyū and Rikyū because of their close association with Nobunaga. It also adds that he paid each master generously. But it was Rikyū, above all, who gave the most pleasure to Hideyoshi, since his tea ceremony had more spiritual depth than Sōkyū's, which was more formal, while Sōgyū's tended toward the more traditional and conservative Kyoto style.

Rikyū had been a pupil of Takeno Jō-ō, and his art was based on *wabi* or the aesthetic of quiet elegance. While he was in Kyoto he leaned the "cabinet" style of the ceremony which was used in large *shoin* rooms. Hideyoshi was interested in all forms of *cha-no-yu*, and Rikyū was able to satisfy his interests better than the other two masters since he was constantly devising new methods of serving tea or new shapes for tea utensils. Before Rikyū's time, for example, most of the bowls used for drinking tea were made either in China or Korea, and they were not designed for the tea ceremony. Rikyū invented the Raku bowl, made from hand-molded earthenware, created specially for serving tea. He selected red and black to go with the green powdered tea, and the weight, shape and rim were all made according to his specifications.

Another important change Rikyū made was in the size of the *fukusa*, or the piece of silk used to handle the valuable tea articles, which he thought too big and clumsy. In the earlier ritual, the *fukusa* was placed in the bosom of the host's kimono or on the cabinet, depending on the style of the ceremony, but Rikyū preferred to fold the silk diagonally and leave it hanging from the host's *obi*, or waistband.

Similarly, Rikyū chose special utensils from among those used in every household, like the bamboo flower vase, and gave it an artistic place in the ceremony of tea. His keen artistic eye and his courage to innovate were good reasons why Hideyoshi and others regarded him as a true master and genius.

Rikyū further distinguished himself by being the only tea master invited by Hideyoshi to the Imperial Palace in 1585. It was at this time that Hideyoshi asked the emperor for permission to bestow on Rikyū the honored title of *koji*, or enlightened recluse, so that he might be allowed to enter the Palace as Hideyoshi's tutor. And so Rikyū's name was formally changed, as it had been on several other occasions during his lifetime.

Rikyū thus advanced from the position of *sadō* to the position of Hideyoshi's closest attendant. He obtained a great deal of power from his relationship with Hideyoshi and was frequently called upon by people for special favors, or to attend tea ceremonies. We can see just how much power he had from a letter written by Hidenaga, the chief counselor of Yamato, who said: "Rikyū will take charge of the household matters, and Hidenaga, the public matters."

It soon began to dawn on Hideyoshi that Rikyū knew too much about household matters, and that he had become insolent in manner. On frequent occasions, Rikyū behaved with great arrogance, a trait which could be attributed to the peculiar brand of self-esteem which the *machi-shū* of Sakai possessed. Hideyoshi was often irritated by Rikyū's clever handling of the difficult tasks that were specially intended to humble him. Many anecdotes are recorded about the clashes between these two men, e.g. Rikyū and his morning glories. Rikyū, who was known throughout the city for his beautiful garden of morning glories invited Hideyoshi to view them early one morning. When the latter arrived, he was surprised to see that all the flowers had been cut, and only when he walked inside the room did he find one morning glory displayed in a vase. Hideyoshi, a proud man by nature, was not amused by his teacher's originality.

On another instance Rikyū recited a poem by Fujiwara no Ietaka which he claimed expressed his own sentiment:

> I would like to show those people
> Looking forward to cherry blossoms
> The green grass hidden in the snow
> In early spring.

This poem was meant to show Hideyoshi that his slightly gaudy tastes were not in accordance with the simplicity and serenity of his teacher's, and Hideyoshi resented the attempt to tell him so.

In the *Record of Yamanoue Sōji* there is a reference to one particular poem by the Buddhist priest Ji Chin, which Rikyū always recited to himself:

> What a pity it is
> That the Pure and Perfect Law
> We should keep unstained,
> Is by men so frequently
> Made a source of worldly gain.

In this poem Rikyū exposed the attitude of those people who used the tea ceremony only as a means of making money. Perhaps these statements were offensive to Hideyoshi, who had done much to promote Rikyū's status as a tea master.

Under these circumstances, and due to some serious rumors that were circulating, Rikyū was ordered to commit suicide. The more immediate reasons for this may have been because Rikyū was selling tea articles, an undignified crime, or that he had encouraged his widowed daughter to refuse Hideyoshi's attentions, or perhaps because he had a statue of himself erected on one of the gates of Daitoku-ji temple. In this case, it is said that Hideyoshi was so enraged at having to walk underneath Rikyū's statue that he ordered the statue to be beheaded as well. Rikyū's sentence of death was seen as penance for having angered his master; in any case, his many enemies, who were jealous of Rikyū's power, saw their objective fulfilled on February 28, 1591, when Rikyū died ceremoniously by his own hand.

Thus the great tea master, who had served Hideyoshi for nine out of his seventy years and Nobunaga twelve, was forced toward a most tragic end. Although it has often been said that Rikyū was responsible for all the rules and ritual of the tea ceremony, it is plain from the historical records that more than one person was involved in the completion of the art of *cha-no-yu*. The final form as we know it today owes its origins not only to the masters Jō-ō and Rikyū, but to the people of Sakai, the samurai lords and their contemporaries. But there is one major difference between the tea ceremony as performed in the days of Rikyū and later ceremonies that followed. The performances of Rikyū were open to men of all classes without distinction, but unfortunately this freedom did not survive his death.

Warriors and the Tea Ceremony

Some people claim that it was Furuta Oribe, his student, who succeeded Rikyū and served Hideyoshi after his death, but it is very uncertain whether this actually occurred or not. According to historical records, two weeks before his death, Rikyū was ordered to return to Sakai and confine himself to his house. Since it was publicly known that Rikyū had been condemned to death, not one of his three thousand students saw him off when he left for Sakai. It is understandable that his students, most of whom were generals and nobles, did not wish to be implicated in his crime and denied having been closely associated with the tea master. There is, however, one letter still in existence which was written by Rikyū to his pupil Matsui Yasuyuki the morning after he reached Sakai. Yasuyuki was chief retainer to Hosokawa Tadaoki, a feudal lord, who later became a tea devotee with the name of Sansai. Rikyū's letter thanked Tadaoki and Oribe for secretly coming as far as Yodo to see him off, a calculated risk in those days but an indication of the strong respect that these two men had for Rikyū.

Just before his death, Rikyū instructed his pupils to learn the art of tea from

Oribe and to learn the making of tea scoops from Sansai. Rikyū was clearly attached to these two students and taught them a great deal of his own techniques. It is improbable, however, that Oribe, a feudal lord, could succeed Rikyū without first resigning his post, which he did only after Hideyoshi's death. Furthermore, there were several other masters in higher positions who would more naturally succeed Rikyū, including Sansai.

It is more likely that Rikyū's post was never filled, for, as we have seen, Hideyoshi quite often conducted the tea ceremony by himself. He was also quite capable of planning such gatherings by himself, although he did obtain assistance from experts in organizing them. But, after Rikyū's death, Hideyoshi was reluctant to show his dependence on the *machi-shū* of Sakai, and he refrained from asking for immediate assistance.

It was to the inhabitants of Hakata that he finally turned for support, especially since he needed the political alliance of the merchants of that town. This was because when Hideyoshi defeated the Shimizu clan of Kyushu in 1587, he captured the town of Hakata on his way back to Osaka. Hakata had been, like Sakai, a self-governing town, whose trade with the merchants of China, including Korea, was established in earlier times. Hideyoshi was eager to conquer China and Korea after his unification of Japan, and he needed the knowledge and economic power of the merchants of Hakata. Therefore, at the "Great Tea Ceremony" of Kitano in 1587, he employed Kamiya Sōtan and Shimai Sōshitsu of Hakata, whom he treated as cordially as his predecessor Nobunaga had treated the men of Sakai when he needed their assistance.

After Rikyū's death, Hideyoshi severed all relations with Sakai and concentrated on Hakata, especially after he declared war on Korea in 1591 when Korea refused to become an ally in his war with China. This war, which lasted seven years, and saw troops dispatched from Japan twice, ended with the death of Hideyoshi and brought about the downfall of the Toyotomi clan. The struggle for control of the country between the Toyotomis and the Tokugawas ended in 1603 with the appointment of Tokugawa Ieyasu as commander-in-chief and shogun. He brought his government to Edo, present-day Tokyo.

Oribe first became acquainted with Ieyasu in 1599, a year after Hideyoshi's death, when he held tea gatherings at Fushimi. It was not until 1605 that he was officially received at Edo to serve Ieyasu's son Hidetada. At this point, Oribe had acquired a considerable reputation as an eminent tea master in Ieyasu's court. Although Oribe followed the rules laid down by Rikyū, his style differed in many ways from that of his master's. Perhaps their differences in background—Oribe was descended from the samurai class, and Rikyū from the merchant class—could account for their differences in taste.

Rikyū's favorite colors were black and gray, while Oribe liked colors which combined dark green and white, or charcoal gray and scarlet on a white background, known later as "Oribe colors." Oribe also preferred a glazed black color, and his favorite shapes were a distorted circle, a triangle or a pentagon, quite distinct from the simple square or circle which Rikyū favored. And while Rikyū tried to maintain a tranquil atmosphere in the garden leading to the tea room, undisturbed even by the scent of flowers, Oribe used to have dandelions blooming or doves singing outside his tea house. While Rikyū had stressed the value of practicality over beauty, Oribe contradicted his dictum by placing more emphasis on appearance than utility.

Oribe might have decided to contravene Rikyū's rules on purpose in an effort to please the public who still regarded Rikyū as a guilty criminal. After the death of Hideyoshi, the tea ceremony underwent more changes, one of the most drastic being its virtual monopoly by the warrior class who looked upon it as a suitable pastime. The Tokugawas especially supported this view, and the hitherto democratic spirit of the tea ceremony was buried together with Hideyoshi.

In keeping with this change, when *cha-no-yu* was no longer the exclusive cult of the court nobles, more importance came to be placed on its outward form. Dignity and decorum correctly observed became fashionable. This concept had its origins in Confucianism, which the Tokugawas adhered to with fervor, and it resulted in a formal and logical arrangement of people and ideas.

Oribe's career was short-lived, and in 1615, during one of the battles between the Tokugawas and the Toyotomis, Oribe, suspected of spying for the latter clan, committed suicide. This put a quick end to his style of tea which combined the *shoin* style of the court nobles with Rikyū's simple tea hut style.

His contemporary, Sansai, did not give lessons, but was a famed collector of tea utensils. An amusing anecdote is told about him. When a certain man asked to see his tea utensils on an appointed day, Sansai decorated the walls of his rooms with the Hosokawa military arms. When asked for an explanation, he replied simply, "I am a warrior, so my principal utensils are weapons of war." Sansai, unlike Oribe, did not attempt to change any of the rules of his teacher. At a later date, he became the patron of Rikyū's son, Dō-an, whom he took into his service.

After Oribe's death, one of his pupils, Kobori Enshū, a feudal lord with a fief of ten thousand *koku*, became famous for his innovations. Although he later succeeded his father as the magistrate for construction and built castles and palaces, like the tower for Nagoya Castle, he was a student of the tea ceremony until the age of twenty-six. He was also a man of many skills. In the historical accounts it is stated that he once danced for many distinguished guests at a cherry-blossom-viewing party. He had also at one time studied meditation under a Zen priest of Daitoku-ji temple called Shunoku Shūon. In this way he was associated with many cultured people and also acquired a broad range of artistic activities. His skill is not only evident in the public buildings he constructed, but also in the tea rooms and gardens around the Daitoku-ji which have been carefully preserved until this day.

Among his many accomplishments, Enshū also designed furniture and tea articles which were distinguished by their dignity and splendor and were referred to as the "Enshū style." This combination of beauty and simplicity came to be known as *kirei sabi*, which resembled the style preferred by the court nobles that Rikyū had frowned upon. But in calligraphy and poetry, Enshū had the same admiration for Fujiwara no Teika as Rikyū had had, and some of the poems in Fujiwara's *Anthology Collected by Imperial Command* were painted on tea bowls by Enshū. His style soon became known as the daimyo style, and his fame spread throughout Japan as Enshū became the shogun's *cha-no-yu* advisor, and many local lords employed his students as their principal tea masters.

The Nobility and the Literati

During the five years of struggle between the Toyotomi and the Tokugawa clans just before the Edo shogunate was established in 1603, the tea ceremony enjoyed great popularity with members of the imperial family and their entourage. The vogue for tea was even reflected in the styles of buildings that were constructed at the time, like the Katsura Imperial Villa in Kyoto, which had a small section in the Shōkintei building that was used exclusively for tea ceremonies. The palace was built by two generations of princes, Toshitada and Toshihito, who was also Hideyoshi's adopted son for a short while. The decoration was elaborate, in the style of tea rooms preferred by the court nobles of the Ashikaga and Muromachi periods. The Shūgaku-in Imperial Villa, also in Kyoto, which followed the above *shoin* style, was constructed specially for the former emperor Gomino-o after the Katsura Villa was built. Similarly, the Minase Shrine, often visited by the emperor, contained a rather splendid room for the tea ceremony.

Perhaps it was Toshihito, Hideyoshi's adopted son, who was responsible for starting up the vogue for tea among the imperial family at the end of the sixteenth century. Toshihito had formerly performed *cha-no-yu* for Hideyoshi, and he later entertained several emperors including Emperor Ogimachi, although it was

47

Hideyoshi who first introduced the tea ceremony to the imperial court. In this way the tea ceremony came to be known by the most powerful regent family, the Konoe clan. The tea styles which they enjoyed most were those of the Oribe School and the Kanamori Sōwa School, because Sōwa used to associate with the former emperors Gosai and Gomino-o, and the latter's wife Tōfukumonin.

Sōwa's style of performance was entirely different from the *wabi* style advocate l by Rikyū and his followers. He preferred a method that was both aesthetic and aristocratic, which pleased members of the nobility who studied with him, such as the other regent clan, the Maeda family of Kaga. One of his students, Prince Joshū-in, who later taught *cha-no-yu* to Konoe Yoraku-in, was referred to by his pupils as the master of the *oryūgi*, or authentic style of tea, while they regarded all other forms contemptuously as *sekenryū*, or popular styles. With this distinct break in the form of the tea ceremony, there evolved a certain snob appeal in the court style of *cha-no-yu*, also known as the daimyo style.

This created a problem for the educated men and priests who did not feel that they belonged to either group. They therefore formed their own style of the tea ceremony in accordance with their status, which was quite close to the daimyo style, since their innovators mingled more with the upper classes. Honami Kōetsu was one of them. Born in 1558, Kōetsu had been a judge and polisher of swords since his youth, but because of his interest in tea, he was a close friend of the tea masters, Oribe, Oda Uraku, Enshū and Sōtan. In view of his profession he mixed with members of the imperial family, court nobles and warriors. He later founded an arts and crafts village at Takagamine in Kyoto and moved there with his family to settle on a piece of land given to him by Tokugawa Ieyasu.

Men like Kōetsu and priests like Shōkadō Shōjō, who served at the Iwashimizu Hachiman Shrine in Kyoto, also had dealings with the court. Shōjō was a noted calligrapher, and during his youth had been employed by Takiyama Sakihisa and Konoe Nobutada with whom he was very close. At the request of Enshū, another close friend, he entertained the imperial family at a tea gathering to improve this relationship. Other influential *cha-no-yu* devotees included priests of Daitoku-ji temple like Takuan (1573–1645) and Kōgetsu, son of Sōgyū, who were both friends of Enshū and Shōkadō.

Sen no Sōtan (1578–1658)

Sōtan was an eminent and respected tea master of the *wabi* style, inherited perhaps from his grandfather Rikyū. It is not certain whether Sōtan was the son of Dō-an, also a well-known tea master, or Shō-an, the stepson of Rikyū after his second marriage. In 1591, when Rikyū committed suicide, Sōtan was only fourteen, and was then staying with his grandfather's Zen teacher Shunoku at the Daitoku-ji. Sōtan practiced Zen meditation, not through any desire to enter the priesthood, but in order to acquire some basic training in Buddhism.

Just about the time when he had finished his studies, Rikyū was punished, and while public hatred for Rikyū mounted to a peak, Sōtan did not feel safe to face the world until three years after the event. He left the temple at seventeen and, according to historical documents, married almost immediately. Once he left the temple, he transferred Rikyū's belongings to another part of Kyoto and, encouraged by his grandfather's large collection of tea utensils, began to learn the tea cult.

As a child Sōtan did not acquire Rikyū's taste for the tea ceremony, and since he did not live together with his grandfather, there was little chance that the two men, separated by over half a century in time, would have much in common in their manner of serving tea. Sōtan came under heavy criticism from some of Rikyū's students who were still alive during that time, and especially from members of the Oribe School whose form of tea ceremony was based on Rikyū's style. In a booklet published by the Oribe School entitled *One Hundred Articles of the Oribe School*, twenty-seven articles were devoted to a condemnation of Sōtan's style. Their main contention was that "Sōtan's tea ceremony was created through his own will and differs greatly from the personal instruction of Rikyū." It was fairly obvious that Rikyū had made a firm impression on his followers and his style was regarded as the criterion for all tea devotees.

Sōtan's personal life was also fraught with strife. He divorced his wife who had given him two sons, Sōsetsu and Sōshu (or Munemori, as he is also called), and toyed with the idea of working for a feudal lord, but since he did not want to live as dangerously as his grandfather had, he soon abandoned the idea. He remarried at the age of forty and lived a life of frugal poverty until his death in 1658. He gave lessons in *cha-no-yu*, but in keeping with his reclusive life, he did not have any distinguished people among his students. As he grew older, his fine upright character and his sincere ideals gained him a great deal of respect among the people of Kyoto, and the four most prestigious tea masters came to study with him. In the *Kakumeiki*, written by the Buddhist priest Hōrin, Sōtan's strict discipline in his style of life was maintained throughout his days. His greatest qualities, kindness and consideration, were later infused with a form of tea ceremony called the "Sōtan style of tea."

One of his pupils, Yamada Sōhen, who later founded the Sōhen School of Tea, took lessons from him when he was eighteen. Sōhen was the heir to the Chōtoku-ji temple, but he was so impressed by his teacher that he gave up his honored position at the age of twenty-six to devote himself to the tea ceremony. There is one anecdote which is very revealing of Sōtan's character. After his decision to become a tea devotee, Sōhen took on his mother's family name and went to live in a small hut in Narutaki, near Kyoto. One day, the chief priest of Hongan-ji temple was to visit Sōhen, and Sōtan, hearing that such a distinguished person was going to see his pupil, rushed over to Sōhen's hut with a water jar and a pair of tongs that had once belonged to his grandfather. He gave his student explicit suggestions as to how to conduct the ceremony, and before the guest arrived, Sōtan hid himself behind a screen for last-minute advice, which Sōhen might have needed.

Another instance of Sōtan's attempts to establish Sōhen's career as *sadō* was when he sent the latter in his place to perform for the daimyo Ogasawara and become his tea master. He boosted Sōhen's confidence by giving him three scrolls of calligraphy which were family heirlooms, and as a result, Sōhen served Ogasawara so ably that he became the tea master to the family for forty-three years.

Sōtan's style of serving tea was also much admired by Sugiki Fusai, another pupil, who was a Shinto priest at Ise Shrine. Fusai later traveled throughout the country spreading the ideas of Sōtan, which differed from the more flamboyant styles of the Oribe and Enshū schools prominent at the time. Above all, Fusai attempted to keep alive the *wabi* tradition which emphasized simplicity through Zen spirituality.

Katagiri Sekishū (1605–73)

Like Sōtan before him, Sekishū was in favor of classic simplicity in tea performances. He was a daimyo and the magistrate of construction for the Tokugawas, like Enshū, but he did not share the same lavish styles in the construction of palaces and gardens which Enshū and Hideyoshi preferred. He studied the art of tea with Kuwayama Sōsen, a pupil of Dō-an, and his mother was the granddaughter of the great tea master Sōkyū, an excellent heritage for a tea devotee.

While he was still practicing Zen meditation at the Daitoku-ji under the guidance of Gyokushitsu Sōhaku, he wrote an important essay on the spirit of tea called *The Essence of Tea* or *Kokoro no Fumi*. He was later employed by the Tokugawa shogunate as their tea instructor. Sekishū followed Rikyū's style, but not in the same way as the Sōtan and Oribe schools, for he felt that a warrior should behave in a manner befitting his rank. He borrowed some of Jō-ō's principles which were more suited to rigid social distinctions, and later wrote down his ideas in a book called *Sekishū's Three Hundred Articles*.

Sekishū's style was influenced by the social conditions of his time, and since the warlike Tokugawas ruled the country, the formal daimyo style was seen to be most suitable for the warrior class. Enshū's style was too extravagant and opulent, although the court nobles preferred it as it reflected their tastes, while Rikyū's simple *wabi* style appealed only to the merchants of Sakai.

The Establishment of Different Schools of Tea

It has been customary since the Heian period in the ninth century for an art to be handed down from one generation to another in the family, to secure the purity of the art from degenerating in any way. At the beginning of the Edo rule, in the seventeenth century, a new custom came into existence, based on the government's policy that the eldest son of a family, whether shogun, lord or merchant, would always succeed his father. This custom was known as *iemoto*, from the same word which stood for an establishment that represented a school of art, although in Edo days *iemoto* was not merely applied to art. In these circumstances a person's lineage came to be more highly regarded than his capability or his skill.

This custom had unhappy repercussions in schools of art, where students, eager to establish their own lineage, would promote their own teachers as the leading representatives of their art. And gradually the original purpose of *iemoto*, which was to protect the different arts, was lost in the scramble to meet the requirements of the system. One natural outcome of this political bias in art was the elevation of tea masters to nobles or feudal lords as they came into close contact with their warrior rulers. These newly dubbed knights were more keen to please their masters than to stick to the strict ethics of tea, and so the *iemoto* system, far from

52

achieving what it set out to do, accomplished just the contrary. The tea ceremony changed its form as many times as the country changed its ruler.

The Senke School of Tea, named after the family name of Sen no Sōtan, was the chief opponent of the Sekishū School, although the influential lords recognized its authority even during Sōtan's lifetime. Sōtan's eldest son, Sōshu, was the chief tea master for the Tokugawas in the Kishu district; Sōshitsu, the second son, was on friendly terms with the Maeda clan; and Sōsa, the youngest, served the Takamatsu family. All three sons lived and worked in Kyoto, giving lessons to the wealthy merchants there, who were beginning to feel socially inferior if they were not well versed in the art of tea.

During this time the Edo administration was becoming more stable politically, and the rule of the samurai gave way to a new system of economic control by the merchant class. As this class played a more dominant role in society than the former warrior class, the tea ceremony once more reverted to a mere pastime for the rich. Tea articles were bought and sold, and marks of authenticity by the more famous masters increased the commercial value of these objects.

But as far as the Senke school was concerned, the art was passed on by Sōtan to his sons, who devoted themselves solely to the cult of tea, unlike the former daimyo tea masters Enshū and Sekishū, who practiced the tea ceremony as a hobby. And in keeping with the prevalent taste of the times, which was for a more lavish drawing room style, the Senke School also developed away from the rigid simplicity of Sōtan toward a looser, more aesthetic style. The Senke School patronized new teachers according to the *iemoto* system, and men like Gensō Sōsa, Joshinsai Tennen, Ittō Sōshitsu and Kawakami Fuhaku (who founded the Edo Senke School) helped formulate the *Seven Important Events of the Tea Ceremony*.

After Sōtan's death in 1658, his school was divided by his three sons, who each started their own school, named according to the area it was situated in. Sōshu called his school the Mushanokōjisenke, after the street by that name in Kyoto;

Sōsa called his the Omotesenke, as it was situated at the front of the house; and Sōshitsu, who inherited the rear of the property, called his school Urasenke.

Matsudaira Fumai and Ii Naosuke

The Sekishū School was popular among the feudal lords because of a rule which said that a student was qualified to teach the tea ceremony once he had completed its course. The Senke School was far more severe when it came to the question of teaching, and many lords preferred the freer method at the Sekishū School. Two students of his developed their own observations and criticisms of the tea ceremony and published important works on the art.

One of them was Matsudaira Fumai (1751–1818), lord of Matsue, a small town, who published a criticism of tea called *Idle Talk* at the age of twenty. He attacked the extravagance of tea performances which ignored the sensitivities and spirituality of an aesthetic art. He was an avid collector of tea articles for he feared that such works of art would perish if they were not carefully preserved. In his *Collection of Valuable Articles in Ancient and Modern Times*, which he wrote between 1704 and 1715, Fumai gave very detailed descriptions of famous tea bowls, tea caddies and ancient silks which belonged to the daimyo families of his period. This is one of the first catalogs of tea articles ever written, and he divides his study into three periods, pre-Rikyū, Rikyū, and post-Rikyū.

At a later date, Fumai wrote down his own observations on the conduct of a tea ceremony in a book called the *Foundation of the Tea Cult*, where he placed great responsibility on the role of the host: "The host is responsible for any mistakes the guest makes. He should entertain the guest according to his mood. If the host sticks too closely to formalities and principles, his service will be regarded as unrefined and in bad taste."

Ii Naosuke (1815–1860) is also known by his tea name of Sōkan. He was the fourteenth child of the lord of Hikone, and when his father died he was forced to live alone in a separate house in the heart of the city. He was then seventeen, and to relieve boredom he took up Buddhism, classical literature and poetry as well as *cha-no-yu*. When his brothers died, he found himself leader of the clan, and at the age of forty-two, he was offered the important office of chief minister by the Tokugawa government. He is also well known as the minister who signed the Commercial Treaty with the United States in 1858.

Sōkan conducted detailed research into the history of tea and wrote prolifically on the spiritual and utilitarian practices of the tea ceremony. He maintained that the spirit of the cult was necessary for the rulers of the country, and although he himself belonged to the daimyo class, his idea of the tea ceremony belonged to the distant age of Rikyū and Sakai, when *cha-no-yu* was simple and accessible to all.

FOOTNOTES

1. Oda Nobunaga (1534–82), a valiant and resolute warrior in the period of the civil wars, almost conquered the whole of Japan by putting an end to the wars, but was attacked by his retainer Akechi Mitsuhide in 1582 and forced to commit suicide.

2. During the Muromachi and Momoyama periods, inhabitants of self-governing cities were referred to by this name.

3. Fujiwara no Teika (1162–1241), a famous poet, scholar and calligrapher of the Kamakura period, compiled the two well-known anthologies entitled *Shinkokin-shū* and *Shinchokusen-shū*.

4. The first rifle from Portugal was imported to Japan through Sakai in 1542.

5. Toyotomi Hideyoshi (1536–98) served under Oda Nobunaga and rose from the rank of a low-class samurai to become ruler of Japan in the Momoyama period. He defeated Mitsuhide, his chief opponent, at the battle of Yamazaki, after which he conquered the remaining areas of Japan left by Nobunaga. In 1585 he became chief advisor to the emperor. He fell ill in 1597, in a battle against Korea, and died a year later.

6. Akechi Mitsuhide (1526–82) was a warrior in the service of Nobunaga, but as he was once humiliated by his master, he attacked Nobunaga at Honnō-ji temple in Kyoto and forced him to commit suicide. Thirteen days later, Mitsuhide himself was defeated at Yamazaki by Hideyoshi.

7. This famous battle, fought in Kyoto between Hideyoshi and Mitsuhide for control of the country after the forced suicide of Nobunaga, ended in June 1582, with the victory of Hideyoshi.

8. Gold and silver mines were discovered in Japan in the sixteenth century, and as a result, tea utensils of that period and after came to be made from these precious metals.

9. Rikyū's name underwent many changes, which A. L. Sadler describes in *Cha-no-yu The Japanese Tea Ceremony*. "Sen no Rikyū was a native of Imaichi in the province of Izumi. His grandfather's name was Sen Ami, an artist, contemporary and intimate friend of Ashikaga Yoshimasa. His father was called Tanaka Yohei . . . Rikyū changed his name from Tanaka to Sen after his grandfather, and first used the title of Sōeki . . ."

10. In the Azuchi and Momoyama periods, tea masters who served samurai and daimyo lords were known by this official name. In the Edo period, *sadō* was a tea master who served the Tokugawas and was usually rewarded with a fief.

11. *Ranjatai* is the highest grade of incense made from aloeswood and sandalwood, first imported from China during the reign of Emperor Shōmu in the eighth century. The incense was stored in the Shōsō-in, the Imperial Treasure House.

56

5. The Tai-an tea house in the grounds of the Myōki-an Zen
temple in Yamazaki, Kyoto.

6. Stepping stones leading into the tea room in the Tai-an.

7. The guests' entrance to the Tai-an tea room.

58

8. The *sōan*-style tea room in the Tai-an shows the rustic style cherished by Rikyū.

9. The simple alcove inside the tea room of the Tai-an.

10. The hanging shelves in one corner of the
Tai-an tea room.

11. Bamboo grillwork in the window next to the
guests' entrance.

12–13. Two pathways in the gardens of the Katsura Imperial Villa, one made of cut stones and the other of natural stones sunk in moss.

14. The New Goten building in the Katsura Imperial Villa.

16. The wall shelves in the First Room of the New Goten.

15. Pebble-lined rain catchments run under the eaves of the New Goten.

17. The Shōkintei houses the principle tea room in the Katsura Imperial Villa.

18. A stone lantern at the pond's edge guides boaters and illuminates the garden at night.

22. The garden of the Ko-hō-an as seen from its re-ception room, or Bōsenseki.

23. A stone wash basin outside the Bōsenseki of the Kohō-an.

24. The combined alcove and preparation area in the Kohō-an tea room.

72

AESTHETICS OF TEA

The Spirit of *Cha-no-yu*

A lot of the misunderstanding of the art of the tea ceremony among Westerners stems from the mistaken impression that it is a purely physical act founded on the custom of drinking tea, or that it is a pleasant pastime when the beverage can be enjoyed among those present. However, this is only the superficial aspect of the tea ceremony and one that is readily noticed. What cannot easily be observed is the spiritual aspect of the ceremony which gives it its name, *cha-no-yu*. Besides a very disciplined frame of mind, which is a prerequisite, there is the special code of ethics shared by the host and guests which makes *cha-no-yu* an art that is distinctly Japanese.

The first tea master of the past to emphasize the spiritual aspect of the tea ceremony was Shukō, who devoted three rules out of the ten he taught to the importance of the right frame of mind. He claimed that purity of mind, rather than an outward appearance of cleanliness, should be observed at all times. In relations between the host and his guests, self-control and consideration should be maintained, and a person of a lower social status should be given the same degree of respect as one who comes from a high social level.

Shukō's ideas were diligently followed by Jō-ō, whose book called *Bunrui Sōjinboku* set down ten out of twelve rules to induce the proper mental attitude while performing the tea ceremony. The tea master's skill, he added, would be enhanced by a correct daily conduct with other people, that is without affectation or arrogance.

These ideas also coincided with Rikyū's, whose words show that he had a great understanding of the deeper spiritual nature of *cha-no-yu*. Once when he was asked about the proper conduct of the host and guest, he answered simply that it is correct for the host to do his best to please his guest, but incorrect to *try* to do so. Unfortunately, Rikyū's simple and unaffected style could not be practiced when he was in the service of Hideyoshi.

After Rikyū's death, the art of *cha-no-yu* was taken over by daimyo lords who pursued it as a means of relaxation from their political lives and as proper recreation befitting their role in society. Nevertheless, Rikyū's influence during his lifetime helped to preserve the purity and simplicity of the tea ceremony from complete deterioration into a fashionable pastime for the feudal chiefs. Even Enshū, who did not receive Rikyū's personal teaching, refused to be entertained with food cooked without sincerity or drink tea from bowls which did not reflect the simplicity (*wabi*) that Rikyū emphasized.

One of Enshū's successors, Katagiri Sekishū, a feudal lord himself, achieved fame as the tutor of the shogun. In his book called *An Essay on Wabi*, he described two types of tea masters: one who loves the formality of the ceremony, the elegance of the atmosphere and the beauty of the utensils; and the true tea devotee who loves the spirituality of the ceremony. Sekishū pointed out that the essence of the *wabi* style of tea can be found in a one-and-a-half-mat room. His ideas clearly differed from the current daimyo style of *cha-no-yu*, but since he himself was a lord, he preached a style of conduct that conformed with one's social standing, contrary to Rikyū, who had stressed the importance of equality in the tea room.

This manner of behavior, however, was carried out by his grandson, Sōtan, and his students. Sōtan, as we know, led a life of austerity, aloof from fame and riches, in pursuit of truth, and gradually, as he won the respect of the people, some of the most famous tea masters of his time began to spread his teachings on *wabi*. Sōtan in his writings deplored the degeneration of *cha-no-yu* at the hands of the nobility, but this only brought further criticism from those whom he attacked, who claimed Sōtan's style of tea was based on egoism and nothing else.

74

After Sōtan's death, his students were appointed chief tea masters to various daimyo families, but they lacked the ability to influence the opinions of the lords, or to bring them back to the *wabi* fold. In addition, the tea ceremony was handed down to the wealthy merchants who had less knowledge about the true spirit of *wabi* and performed the ceremony according to their own uninitiated styles.

Some feudal lords like Matsudaira Fumai, who had studied the Sekishū style of tea, criticized the degeneration of *cha-no-yu*. In his books he pointed out that the ceremony was diverging from its former theory and was being performed in all sorts of ways. Tea masters only talked of *wabi* but did not practice the elements of the style. He called for a return to the original concept of tea, since mere mastery of ritual was insufficient if the basic rapport between host and guest remained undeveloped. In like manner, Ii Naosuke, author of the well-known book on tea *Ichie-shū*, described the ceremonies of his time as lacking in proper communication between host and guest.

It is interesting to note the two daimyo tea masters' approach to tea, which was a combination of social entertainment with personal pleasure. The tea ceremony seemed to have lost forever the humble *wabi* style as it progressed from the time of Shukō to Naosuke, despite Fumai's warning against an excessive show of materialism in the ceremony. Not until the latter half of the nineteenth century, when Okakura Kakuzo (or Tenshin) wrote *The Book of Tea* in the English language, was another attempt made to capture the elusive "spirit" of tea. He said:

> Tea with us became more than an idealisation of the form of drinking; it is a religion of the art of life. The beverage grew to be an excuse for the worship of purity and refinement, a sacred function at which the host and guest joined to produce for that occasion the utmost beatitude of the mundane. The tea-room was an oasis in the dreary waste of existence where weary travellers could meet to drink from the common spring of art-appreciation.

Thus the intricacy of thought behind the tea ceremony is expressed, without which the essence of the performance is lost.

Wabi and Other Terms in the Tea Ceremony

The literal translation of *wabi* is apology, with an added sense of worry, although the word contains the idea of simplicity as well. Since the middle of the Muromachi period, two other words have been coined to mean simplicity and tranquillity, *hiekareru* and *kajikeru*, which have come to be used interchangeably with *wabi*.

The term *kareru* in the tea ceremony was defined by Shukō, who applied it to masters who not only owned artistic utensils, but also had the ability to appreciate their beauty. He discussed the term *kareru* while criticizing the trend for using Bizen and Shigaraki pottery by those who had no knowledge of their artistic value. This indicated a gradual change in the aesthetic sense, and those learning the art began to be more discriminating in the types of tea articles they used. It was not until later, at the end of the Muromachi period, that the expression *wabi-suki* was substituted for *kareru*.

For a *wabi* style to be correctly effected, the tea master should live a life of seclusion in the countryside, as far away from the center of the city as possible, where his inner quietude could not be adversely influenced by more worldly matters. It was said that a life without embellishments of any kind was the best means of attaining spiritual satisfaction. This idea is based on the Buddhist tenet of a life of detachment without the isolation of a hermit. This concept had great influence among the merchants of Sakai who learned *cha-no-yu* and who could detach themselves from daily commercial activities through the tea ceremony.

It is also said that the man who believes implicitly in *wabi* casts away everything that is unnecessary except for those requirements which are essential to practical living. To observers from the outside, his life may seem frugal and miserable, but for the true adherent, it is the attainment of a peaceful frame of mind in the transience of the temporal world. Very few men, it seems, could put this ideal into practice, and the *Record of Yamanoue Sōji* speaks of only one master, Zempō, who was a true follower of *wabi*.

Rikyū comes very close to Zempō in his ideas on the tea ceremony, especially in his invention of the one-and-a-half-mat tea room where *cha-no-yu* could be performed with the same spirituality as in a larger room. His love of dark, somber colors such as gray and black, and his preference for rough Raku tea bowls is exemplary of the *wabi* spirit. But Rikyū, who served the powerful rulers Nobunaga and Hideyoshi, could not practice this ideal, although he taught the *wabi* style to his students. He regretted this state of affairs where he had to contravene the ideals of the tea ceremony in order to stay alive, and often consoled himself with Fujiwara's poem (see page 42).

The meaning of *wabi* underwent a change during the Edo period, when more stress was placed on the idea of simplicity alone, without tranquillity or solitude to complete its meaning. There is another word, *iki*, which was popular during that time and was thought to convey the same feeling as *wabi*, but *iki* has connotations of luxury hidden in its meaning and stems from a kind of epicurism. The concept of *wabi* is exceptionally difficult, even to the Japanese, for although *wabi* utensils are visually discernible, it is the feeling that is most difficult to convey correctly.

Zen Philosophy and the Tea Ceremony

It was the Zen priest Eisai who first brought powdered green tea to Japan and encouraged tea-drinking among his fellow priests. He planted tea bushes around his temple in an effort to achieve this end, as well as to spread Zen teachings in Japan. This early connection between Zen religion and the tea ceremony encouraged other tea masters to study Zen philosophy, although this could hardly be avoided at the time since the only teachers of the ceremony were the Zen priests. A lot of the preparations involved are a reflection of Zen thought, so much so that in later days the expression "Zen and Tea are one and the same" came to be used. Yamanoue Sōji even went further in saying that since *cha-no-yu* derived from Zen, it was obligatory for all tea masters to study the philosophy. Shukō, the father of the tea ceremony, studied Zen under the monk Ikkyū of Daitoku-ji temple, and his chief disciple by the name of Yōsō Sōi spread Zen teachings to the merchants of Sakai. He was very popular among them, and the first Zen temple was built in Sakai called the Nanshū-ji, where Shukō was invited to become the first chief abbot.

The close ties between the merchants of Sakai and the Zen priests were further cemented when two wealthy Sakai merchants, Takeno Jō-ō and Kitamuki Dōchin, both well-known tea masters, studied Zen under Dairin Shūtō, who had been Rikyū's tutor. His other teachers were the priests Shōrei Shōkin and Kokei Sō-chin.

When the Daitoku-ji had to be restored after it was partly destroyed during the civil wars, it was the merchants of Sakai who helped to finance the project. It soon became the custom to appoint one abbot for both temples, and each time this occurred the merchants donated a substantial sum to both temples. This interdependence between priests and the *machi-shū* made it easy for many merchants and their sons to become priests at the Daitoku-ji—for instance Sengaku Shutō, son of the merchant Tani Sōin. The thirteenth abbot of Nanshū-ji and the 156th of Daitoku-ji was the son of Tsuda Sōgyū, called Kōgetsu Sōgan. Chiefly as a result of the spiritual and financial reliance between these two classes of people, many merchants who were tea devotees began to learn Zen, even when they had no intention of entering religious life.

Perhaps another factor which explains the close relationship between Zen and *cha-no-yu* is found in the development of the fine arts, such as calligraphy, painting and pottery, which were started by Zen priests. The first scrolls (*kakemono*) to hang in the tea room alcove were specimens of highly prized calligraphy done by the Sung and Yuan priests of China. These scrolls were also hung in Zen temples, for the priests had great respect for the Chinese Zen monks. It was not until Jō-ō's time that the same kind of scrolls were painted by Japanese priests, and used to decorate the alcoves of tea rooms. Rikyū used to decorate his tea room with his teacher Kokei's calligraphy, a great honor for the latter since it was more usual for writing to be admired posthumously. Kokei created special one-line writings called *ichigyōsho* and inscriptions on the top of scrolls called *gasan* specifically for tea rooms, and they were known by the name *chagake*.

The close affinity between Zen teachings and the tea ceremony helped mold the rules and ritual in the development of *cha-no-yu*, and the simplicity and purity inherent in the religion influenced the form of the tea ceremony. In effect, the same harmony of mind which could only be attained upon entering the gate of a Zen temple could now be achieved in the serene atmosphere that pervades the tea room.

The love of the tea ceremony among the priests resulted in the building of many smaller temples in the precincts of the Daitoku-ji where tea gatherings could be held. A good many priests developed a profound aesthetic sense and collected beautiful tea utensils which became valuable tea items. But this was not common practice in all temples, many of whose abbots frowned on the tea ceremony, which they regarded as a pleasant pastime favored by the wealthy, and forbade their priests from participating in it.

In my opinion, although there is a very close relationship between the ethics of Zen and *cha-no-yu*, they differ in the following manner: while Zen calls for enlightenment of the individual through meditation and detachment, *cha-no-yu* is an art in which people communicate with each other through sincerity of spirit and purity of mind.

Harmony with Nature

Harmony with nature forms the essential basis of *cha-no-yu*, for it is regarded by its originators as the best means of awakening aesthetic appreciation. The special styles of tea houses and gardens are an indication of this ideal, and unlike Western homes and gardens which are built to contrast with nature, Japanese tea rooms and gardens are designed to blend in harmoniously with their natural surroundings.

Tea houses can be made from wooden logs with their bark still intact, or unpolished wooden pillars naturally bent with age, and their walls plastered with mud, a perfect echo of nature at its most ordinary. In the gardens, natural-shaped stones are used to build paths and rock gardens, and tea arbors are built next to large trees to give them a more rustic setting. The kind of weather, the movement of the sun in a day's passing, and the change of seasons all play a major role in this duet with nature.

The Japanese have always observed nature very closely, and this preoccupation with the change of seasons influenced the oldest anthology of poems compiled at the end of the Nara period, the *Manyōshū*. Those who found aesthetic enjoyment in the tea ceremony also possessed great sensitivity toward nature, and undoubtedly the tea ceremony came to become closely associated with the passing of the seasons; a significant part of the ritual lies in the variation of tea utensils, flowers, the special meal (*kaiseki*), cakes, and so on, in accordance with the different months of the year.

I think it is appropriate here to give a brief description of these changes based on nature, starting with the first ceremony of the year. On New Year's Day, the tea ceremony starts with *ōbuku-cha*, which literally means "good luck tea." On the fifth or sixth day it is the custom for the students to assemble at their teacher's house to celebrate the first kettle, or *hatsugama*. If there is snow on the ground, the snow will be boiled to make tea, and often poems are composed at these meetings to reflect the tranquillity of snow.

In January and February, the evenings are long and dark, and special evening gatherings can take place called *yobanashi*, which are distinguished by the use of very valuable tea articles. Special flowers are selected to match the mood of the *yobanashi*, like winter camellias, white plum blossoms, petunias, winter peonies and primroses. The meal eaten at the start will include lobster, sillago or sea bream, which are winter delicacies.

A special spring gathering is held the day before the spring equinox, which is calculated according to the lunar calendar, where the theme is a longing for spring. In this case, a dawn ceremony called *akatsuki*, which might take place at four in the morning before the sun rises, is held with pink plum blossoms and heath roses for the floral decoration. For the meal, wild plants such as bracken, horsetails, butterbur flowers and some green vegetables are served. The emphasis is always on the coming of spring, and bowls with symbolic designs of lingering snow, thin icicles, field fires, sprouting plants and flowers, or nightingales are used to convey this feeling.

In March and April the cold weather thaws and spring returns with the first flowers appearing after the bleak winter. Cherry blossoms decorate the tea room during the day, and tea devotees gather round the kettle set outside under the trees to admire the cherry blossoms at dusk.

May and June are months of warmth, and tea gatherings called *yūzari* are held indoors in the evenings when the portable charcoal brazier (*furo*) replaces the "firing pit" (*ro*), a symbol that summer is near.

In the months of July and August, the two hottest months of the year, tea ceremonies can be held at dawn before the sun becomes too hot for comfort. Occasionally people perform *cha-no-yu* outdoors, for instance in the mountains or at the riverside where it is cool and breezy.

The portable brazier used for the summer months is stored away in October, and the mood of lingering summer is evoked through the use of sober-colored tea articles and the arrangement of autumn flowers in the alcove. As the days get colder, and before the built-in hearth or fire pit is opened, the charcoal brazier is moved closer to the guests. This custom, when the brazier is moved to the center of the tatami mat, is called *naka-oki*.

In November, the fire pit which is built into the floor is opened and the tatami mats are replaced by new ones. It is also the custom during this time to open a new tea container and serve the guests with fresh tea. This once again changes the mood of the tea house, while in the garden, new, green bamboo fences replace the old ones and the rain pipes of the house are replaced by newly cut bamboo pipes. This renovation is done very solemnly and is regarded by tea masters as symbolic of the new year.

There are tea gatherings held in December to share the sorrow of parting with the old year, and to aspire toward greater things to come in the new. These personal sentiments are reflected in the choice of tea articles according to the feelings of the host, and in general the last month of the year is usually a busy one, amid the preparations for the change of calendar.

In the seasonal variations mentioned above, it is obvious that the most important aspect of these changes lies in the choice of special tea utensils to fit the different moods that are created. The emphasis in earlier tea ceremonies tended toward the precious and the luxurious, but as the spiritual essence of the event came to be understood, a taste for simplicity was acquired. Masters like Zempō had a certain influence in this change, and in his *Essay on Sarugaku* he had this to say: "Indeed *temae* with a gold brazier, kettle and water jar is splendid, but it does not make any impression on the mind. But if the rough earthenware from Ise or Bizen is used, it is the heart which will be deeply satisfied." This is the profound, aesthetic sentiment which the tea utensils are supposed to instill in the beholder.

Yet the individual beauty of each utensil must also blend harmoniously with all the other utensils needed for the ceremony, which are in turn selected according to the demands of the occasion or the time of year. There are three basic principles involved in the decoration of a tea room (that is, placing flowers in the vase, hanging the scroll in the alcove and putting the kettle on the fire), and they are based on time, place and rank. Time means the consideration of the season in which the tea ceremony is held and the purpose of the occasion. Place means the consideration of the space and atmosphere of the room and the choice of articles which that entails, while rank denotes the ability and knowledge of the tea master, which must be suited to the location and the kind of ceremony that is given.

It would not be appropriate, for instance, to choose a scroll, albeit a favorite summer scene, for a winter tea ceremony, for the discord will not instill any meaningful feeling into the occasion. But in rare cases, and when done by a very skilled tea master, a painting showing snow and ice, or a piece of calligraphy expressing cold-weather scenes, can create a feeling of coolness in the hot summer.

A harmonious arrangement of tea utensils depends a great deal on the variety of shapes of the different vessels used. Unlike the Western habit of matching cups or bowls in sets which are identical, Japanese aesthetics is based on the charm of variety, where no two articles will be exactly the same. If a tall tea caddy is used, it will be balanced by a flat water jar, while a round kettle will be used on a square brazier.

At times the tea master will even avoid using two articles produced in the same region or made of the same material, since this overlap (*tsuku*) might be regarded as carelessness on the part of the master. On the other hand, if three articles which come from the same district are used, this is permissible since it indicates emphasis on the particular choice, but four will be excessive.

Antique utensils dating from the Muromachi period are still used today for formal ceremonies. Articles produced during the Edo period are considered as contemporary pieces, and they are usually harmoniously combined with antiques in an ordinary tea gathering.

Another factor governing the grouping of tea articles is the *mei* utensils. The name *mei* is used for any favorite item owned by the tea master, and this idea stems from the early days when only highly prized utensils would be called *mei* by their owners, but now any spoon or bowl can be known as *mei* if they are a favorite art object for the tea master. The setting of different kinds of *mei* together can help to express a season or theme, and also gives the ceremony a more personal flavor.

And lastly, there is the decoration of the tea room itself, which is an important reflection of harmony with nature. In historical times, the *dōbōshū* of the shogun Ashikaga would hang two or three scrolls in the alcove of the *shoin* tea room. They discovered a fundamental principle in the use of the wall space based on the Chinese theory of *yin* and *yang*, in order to determine the correct spacing between the scrolls and the height of the scrolls in relation to the height of the room. They called their theory *kanewari*, which meant the wall space was divided into six sections by drawing five lines. In the middle of each of the six sections they drew one line; the first five lines were considered *yang*, or positive; and the other six lines drawn in later were *yin*, or negative. This rule was also applied to the decoration of the shelves in the side alcove, the design of the stationery desk of the *shoin* rooms and the arrangement of tea utensils, and was incorporated into the aesthetics of the tea ceremony. In practical terms this meant that the number of utensils placed in the main alcove must never be the same as those in the side alcove, and if the former are even in number, then the latter must be odd in number, otherwise the *yin-yang* balance between the two sections will be disturbed.

The Creative Mind
Although harmony and aesthetics are both necessary in the art of the tea ceremony, it is not complete without the application of a creative sense known as *hataraki*,

kanawari

without which the act of preparing and serving tea becomes dull and prosaic. In the *Record of Yamanoue Sōji* (in which this creativity is known as *sakui*), there are two distinct parts to *cha-no-yu*: one where tradition must be observed in the ritual, and the other where pure imitation is to be substituted by an openness of approach, in other words, a sense of creativity. Another *Book of Tea* written in 1600 by Sōshun-ō states that while a certain conservatism is necessary, the ceremony should not lack in originality of thinking or become stiff and static.

The historical records of *cha-no-yu* gatherings show how this sense of creativity has evolved. In early times, the custom was to begin the tea ceremony after the room had been decorated with all the adornments and the meal served. Some time later, a small change was made, and the alcove was only filled with a few chosen items. The host would bring in the other articles as the ceremony progressed. Later, the guests were made to rest in another room while the host changed the arrangement of the tea room and prepared the thick tea served to the guests when they returned. Thus an element of freshness in the ceremony was maintained.

The creativity of the host was expressed in his choice of furnishings for the tea room and in the use of articles he preferred without imitating others. One variation which resulted in the quest for originality was the hanging of the flower vase from the wall instead of placing it on the floor of the alcove.

An anecdote which best illustrates the origins of *hataraki* is told by Matsuya Hisamasa, who was invited to a gathering given by Jō-ō in 1542. In those days it was customary to display only one item in the alcove, so a messenger was sent to Hisamasa to ask him which he preferred: a painting of waves or the display of a prized tea container. It so happened that Hisamasa and his fellow guest did not agree on the choice, so Jō-ō, in a diplomatic and original move, displayed both items in the alcove to please his guests.

Yamanoue Sōji would have approved of Jō-ō's inventiveness provided that he did not become too creative, which would have disrupted the subtlety of the tea ceremony, or that he did not repeat it more than twice in every ten performances. Had the idea been someone else's, then it would have been unimpressive for Jō-ō to have imitated it.

The creativity in *cha-no-yu* cannot be taught, it is inbred. A pupil of Rikyū once asked the master about the mysteries of the tea ceremony, to which Rikyū replied: "You suggest a feeling of coolness in summer, and cosiness in winter; when you burn charcoal you see that the water boils, when you make tea you see that it tastes good. There is no other secret." His pupil seemed unsatisfied with this enigmatic reply since it was obvious that anyone could do this, to which Rikyū replied that if such a man did exist, he would willingly learn from him.

Tea masters usually advised their pupils to think for themselves, for apart from teaching them the ritual of the tea ceremony, it was impossible to train their minds or increase their creativity. For this reason, Zen inscriptions are often chosen to decorate tea rooms, for it is essentially the Buddhist creed of enlightenment through self-knowledge that can guide the student to think independently.

There is another story often told about the tea master Sugiki Fusai and one of his pupils who asked for something to remind him of his teacher's instructions. After some thought Fusai took a piece of burning charcoal from the fire pit, put it into a small portable brazier and handed it to his pupil, saying, "I have nothing else to offer you, but take this home and put it in your hearth and keep it burning by performing *cha-no-yu* morning and evening. If you can keep this up, you will understand all that I have taught you." In other words Fusai's advice was to show his student that he can only learn through his own devices, for only through practice can the novice discover the mysteries of the art.

Another tea master, Joshinsai, based his teachings on one maxim which was: "Conduct the tea ceremony steadily, but modestly, and avoid any behavior that is both showy and affected." He left it to his pupils to find out, through experience, just what the best type of conduct was. And it is this sense of creativity, which

86

stems from Zen philosophy, that prevented the tea ceremony from becoming a mundane, ritualistic art, and it is the most personal expression in the overall characteristics of *cha-no-yu.*

Invitation to a Tea Ceremony

To the Japanese the custom of drinking tea is a formal affair with roots that spring from an inherited past that has influenced the habits and manners of the people. To those who are not acquainted with what may seem to be a strange and unfamiliar pastime, let us make an imaginary visit to a Japanese home to find out.

When paying a visit to a close friend it is polite to telephone first and arrange a convenient time in which to call, otherwise he may not have enough time to make the necessary preparations. Once you are there, you remove your shoes before stepping into the house, and arrange them neatly at the entrance, as is the Japanese custom. For a tea ceremony gathering the footwear is usually placed on the *tobi-ishi* or stepping stones that lead up to the guests' entrance. It is considered improper either to wear an overcoat or to carry a handbag when entering a tea room, since this denotes a lack of respect for the host. It is therefore advisable to leave all these belongings on the porch (*yoritsuki*) in the basket provided.

In the tea room, the seat in front of the alcove is reserved for the guest of honor, and a few articles might be all that it contains. This may look bleak, but it is specially decorated in this fashion, so that each item is prominently displayed and can be admired by the guest. The decoration is not repeated for later occasions.

When food is served, it will not cover the entire dish, since the container itself is an object of art to be appreciated by the guest. Great pains are taken to ensure that tea articles and ordinary containers are displayed to the fullest extent for their artistic value. The *kaiseki* meal consists of several dishes brought out one at a time rather than all at once. The host will appreciate comments made on the beauty of the tea articles or the flavor of the food. The *kaiseki* food is served in an attractive way, cut into unusual shapes or adorned with flowers, and is specially prepared for the occasion.

In a *cha-no-yu* gathering, everything that is seen and used should be an object of appreciation, and this applies not only to precious or famous objects but to everyday utensils as well. This attitude is a reflection of *taru-o-shiru*, meaning "to know what is enough," and it stems from the *wabi* tea style, where beauty is found in the imperfect and the ordinary as well as in the perfect. This attitude permeates the Japanese character; it induces a peacefulness of mind and allows its followers to act calmly and naturally, without conflict.

TEMAE

The Origin and Meaning of *Temae*

Social evenings during the Heian period of the ninth century were highlighted by popular games devised by the nobility for their own amusement, including the competition of incense-smelling mentioned earlier, and *monoawase*, a simple card game involving the pairing off of different kinds of shells, insects, flowers or grass. As social activities increased through the ages, the nature of these games became more complex and special rules and procedures were set up.

In the same way the tea ceremony also became more complex as new rules were invented to enhance these evenings, and gradually the nature of *cha-no-yu* changed. The first major contribution toward this change was the manufacture of Japanese tea utensils, which had previously been imported from China. But other *temae* rules soon followed, depending on whether the ceremony was conducted indoors or out on the lawn, and many new kinds of tea articles were added to the original set.

Some of the reasons for the changes in *temae* over the centuries were historical and sociological, depending on the social class which engaged in the tea ceremony, for its own customs and traditions were infused into *temae*. And during the Edo period, when the *iemoto* system was introduced for all the professions, special schools passed on their individual techniques to their students, and in this way more types of *temae* were created.

Temae is the etiquette of making and serving tea, a step-by-step procedure of the tea ceremony which can be memorized much in the same way as learning the steps of a dance. When *temae* is performed before large audiences and the host becomes the center of attention, the real meaning of the action is lost in the spectacle. It is not, as is commonly believed, the means and end of the tea ceremony, but *temae* has a deeper and more subtle aspect which is only apparent when it is properly performed.

The earliest origins of *temae* were founded on the actions of the *dōbōshū*, the lord's attendant, whose duty was to handle valuable utensils carefully and to serve tea in a graceful manner. In the course of time, small tea gatherings among commoners became popular where the host himself made the tea. The host's movements while making tea became an important aspect of the event and served to entertain his guests. Thus the specific name *temae* was given to this performance.

The originator of *temae* was Shukō, who taught the deep spiritual meaning of the tea ceremony to his pupils. This was done by concentrating the mind on the gestures, rather as in a meditative exercise. Shukō also taught them how to behave inconspicuously and unaffectedly, and these ideas became the essence of *temae*. And gradually as the ceremony became less complex, the rules of *temae* were simplified at the same time.

There are three basic elements present in the concept of *temae*, which are arrangement, purification, and calmness of mind. Arrangement includes everything from carrying the utensils into the tea room to setting them down properly. When these are brought into the room one by one they can be admired individually from a small distance, and they are so arranged that their beauty can be admired from many different angles. The element of surprise would be lessened if they were brought in all at once, and this is usually avoided in a proper tea ceremony.

Purification is the act of cleaning the tea bowl, caddy and tea scoop. Warming the bowl with hot water and wiping it is a standard cleaning preparation, but the custom of passing a piece of silk over the tea caddy and scoop is a formality that has been handed down from the *dōbōshū*. The silk used to clean the tea caddy symbolizes a cleansing and purification of the mind, which if done without pretension induces a feeling of peace and tranquillity in the guests.

This calmness of feeling can be disrupted if the tea master is too quick in his actions or too hurried in his pace. After the cakes have been served, a short space of time should elapse, giving the guests an opportunity to admire the hanging scroll and the vase of flowers. During this time, the tea is made and then served to the guests, who drink it and pass the bowl back to the host. He then rinses it and begins to put all the articles away, smoothly and without hurry. Thus *temae* comes to an end, lasting some twelve or thirteen minutes in all, leaving the guests with a feeling of contentment and satisfaction at having partaken in a tranquil ceremony.

Different Types of *Temae*

Temae can be divided into three main types: the *shoin* style, the *sōan* style and the *hiroma* style.

The *shoin*-style *temae* makes use of a cabinet called *daisu*, which has an upper and lower shelf on which all the utensils used for the tea ceremony are placed. The host conducts the preparations with utmost solemnity and in strict accordance to the rules which etiquette calls for. It is also stated that his mind should be free of all mundane thoughts while he is performing the ceremony. Although there are more than sixty variations of the *shoin* style *temae*, the three principle ones are known as *koshiki*, *shin*, and *gyō*.

The *sōan* style differs from the above in its basic concept of the host's duty, which is to serve his guests in a less formal ceremony. The host and his guests sit facing one another across the fire pit, or *ro*, and the tea is drunk from rustic utensils that are used in the *wabi* style of tea ceremony. The host himself brings out the different utensils one by one as the ceremony progresses, and only the tea caddy, kettle, water jug and brazier are placed in the room beforehand. This procedure is known as *hakobidate*, and distinguishes the *sōan* from the *shoin* style.

The *hiroma* or large room style evolved during the Edo period and is by far the most regulated of the three types and most suited for very large gatherings of people. The design of the room is different: the alcove is decorated in a special way, and shelves have to be built into the room to hold all the utensils. The host also uses two tea bowls at the same time to ensure that the tea is properly prepared. These bowls are given a special name—*kasane jawan*.

Some other styles which I shall mention briefly are the *kinindate*, which is related to the *hiroma* style except that it is only performed for exalted individuals; the *chasenkazari* and the *shomō mono*, where the host asks the principal guest to arrange the flowers for the alcove; and the *shichijishiki temae*, where several people can act as hosts or guests, and special instructions are drawn from a box called *orisue*. This style of *temae* is performed in silence since its chief purpose is to attain unison of action among those present. There is even one style which requires everyone to sit on chairs (*ryūrei*), and another only performed outdoors (*nodate*), and one where all the utensils are placed in a box (*chabako*).

The Order of *Temae*

Despite the different types of temae used in tea ceremonies today, there are certain basic rules which are common to all, as in the following.

ARRANGEMENT OF UTENSILS
Tea utensils must be arranged in a way that facilitates their removal and re-placement. Depending on the type of *temae* followed during the ceremony, when some utensils are taken out for use and others left for decoration, great care must go into the planning and arrangement so that everything functions smoothly during the performance.

WIPING THE UTENSILS
The cleaning of the tea caddy which holds the tea and the tea scoop (*chashaku*) is

an important act for it signifies a spiritual cleansing of the mind and heart, when all thoughts pertaining to the temporal world should be dismissed. When making *koicha* or thick tea, the tea caddy is wiped first with a folded piece of silk cloth called the *fukusa*, and in the preparation of *usucha*, thin tea, the special lacquered tea caddy is also wiped with the *fukusa*.

WARMING THE TEA WHISK AND TEA BOWL

The tea whisk (*chasen*) is made of freshly split bamboo and should be warmed first, when it should be checked to see if all the strands are intact. The tea bowl should also be warmed since a cold bowl does not produce good tea. Both are done at the same time by pouring hot water into the tea bowl and immersing the whisk in it. The bowl is then wiped dry with a *chakin* or white linen cloth.

MAKING THE TEA

This is the most important part of the tea ceremony, for although *temae* is a necessary preliminary, it will be performed in vain if the tea in the end does not taste good. As we all know, the quality of tea depends on the correct proportion of boiling water and tea. In making *koicha* (thick tea), three heaped tea scoops (3.5 grams) of tea is required per person, and in *usucha* (thin tea), only half that amount is needed. It is said that the best *koicha* results when the correct amount of tea for three to five persons is made at the same time in the tea bowl.

When boiling water is added to the tea in the bowl, the mixture is stirred with the tea whisk, and here again the procedure is different for *koicha* and *usucha*. In the case of thick tea, the whisk is moved slowly and smoothly, just enough to turn the tea into a thick liquid. Any rapid movements will make the tea too thick. In *usucha*, the whisk is worked back and forth quickly until a foam appears, perhaps after fifteen to twenty strokes. Too much stirring will produce a foamy tea and too little will make the tea watery, so the best way to begin might be to practice stirring with a bamboo whisk to find out how many strokes are needed for *usucha*.

In making *koicha*, the amount of water added to the powdered tea makes a great deal of difference in both the taste and the consistency. If too little water is added, it will be impossible to achieve the right texture, and if more water is added to this later on, the taste will suffer. In the olden days it was said that if you had not mixed the equivalent of one *kanme* (8 lbs.) of powdered tea, then you could not make proper *koicha*. At the rate of one tea ceremony held for five persons once a week, this would mean that one would have to practice this art for five years before producing a good cup of tea!

The temperature of the hot water used is another factor that will determine whether or not the tea will taste good. This is dependent on the season, and small adjustments are made to accommodate for changes in weather. In spring, for example, one ladle of cold water is added to the kettle just before the tea is made to reduce the water's temperature slightly. In winter, when the fire pit is used, boiling water is poured straight into the tea bowl.

It is also necessary to use fresh tea, as the color and flavor of tea change when it is kept in a container that is not properly sealed. On very humid days, moisture forming in the tea can change the flavor, so the best method is to use fresh tea for these ceremonies, for after all the important factor is to serve the guests with the tastiest tea.

WASHING THE BOWLS AND THE WHISK
After tea is drunk, the bowls are handed back to the host, who fills them with a little hot water to wash them. He also dips the tea whisk in hot water and returns the utensils to the area where *temae* was performed. When the guest says to the host, "Please put it away," he returns the bowls to their proper place and the ceremony comes to an end.

WIPING THE TEA SCOOP AND REPLACING THE UTENSILS
When the tea bowls are put away, the tea scoop is wiped with the *fukusa* and placed

in its original position. The host will then put all the tea utensils he used for the ceremony back where they belong, and he does this at a normal pace, neither too hurriedly nor too slowly. There are variations in the speed of his movements throughout the ceremony, and a good host is one who does not bore his guests, whose interest in his performance should be maintained throughout. When the ceremony is over, the guest will come away feeling satisfied with both the excellent tea and the performance.

A Look at Tea Utensils

When the tea has been drunk and all the other utensils put away, the host covers the water jar with a lid to signify the end of the ceremony. At this point the guest may ask the host for permission to examine the articles used.

If *usucha* was served, the chief guest will ask to see the lacquered tea caddy, called *natsume*, and the tea scoop, and if *koicha* was served, he will ask the host for the tea caddy known as *cha-ire*, the tea scoop and the bag which held the caddy.

The chief guest places these utensils before the others for their observation, after which he returns them to the place where *temae* was performed. The host, in the meantime, waits outside the room or area where the utensils are stored, closing the sliding doors so that the guests can peruse them at peace.

When the guests have looked at the different items, they return them to their original places, and this is the signal for the host to reenter the room. He then carries the utensils away with him. This is also the time when conversation between the host and guests usually starts, perhaps with a question about the tea scoop. In formal tea ceremonies, this part forms an integral step in the whole performance, and the host will only use articles that will provoke interested queries from the guests. If no questions are asked, it is a sign that the spirit of the ceremony has not pervaded the guests.

Etiquette for the Guest

Since the tea ceremony is such a formal and conventional affair, there are also special rules to be observed by the guest. These are briefly listed below.

ATTIRE

Fifty years ago, the only clothing habitually worn to a tea gathering was the kimono, but nowadays, when the Japanese wear Western clothes most of the time, it is no longer obligatory to wear formal kimono complete with family crest, or *hakama*, a divided skirt over the kimono, or *jittoku*, a short kimono coat worn over the formal one, though a long kimono coat is not permissible. For a man dressed in Japanese clothes, a clean pair of divided socks (*tabi*) should be worn for the ceremony. A woman, if not clad in kimono, should wear a dress or skirt that covers her knees when she is kneeling, and a clean pair of white socks over her stockings. Jewelry and other accessories are normally removed beforehand for fear of damaging the fine tea utensils. It is also better not to wear perfume which would jar with the smell of incense and spoil the ambience of the tea room—an essential factor of the ceremony.

PERSONAL ITEMS

It is appropriate for the guest to bring a folding fan (*sensu*), not for cooling himself, but to use for greeting his host and other guests. The *tenugui*, or long handkerchief, used to wipe his hands before entering the tea room should be brought by the guest. He should also bring a piece of thin tissue paper called *kaishi* to wipe his mouth after he has eaten the sweets, or to wipe the rim of the tea bowl, and *kobu-kusa*, a small piece of brocade on which to rest his tea bowl when he drinks the tea.

BEHAVIOR

It is considered impolite to be late for a small *cha-no-yu* gathering that is set for an appointed time. When a large number of guests have been asked to a day-long ceremony it is not important to arrive on time, but in the former case it is good manners to arrive twenty minutes before the ceremony starts.

It is not proper to enter rooms other than the room where the tea ceremony is to be held. Usually places which are prohibited to the guests are shown by placing a small stone over the stepping stone, or a bamboo pole across the entrance to a room or to a garden path. When walking through the garden it is advisable to make use of the stepping stones to avoid trampling on the moss or grass.

Smoking is generally prohibited at these gatherings, and the smoking box or *tabako bon* is a decorative item, since the ash in its tray has been leveled off and properly arranged. Sometimes there are designated places for the guests to smoke and they can do so by asking their host's permission.

It is customary to maintain absolute silence during the ceremony when the guest is expected to observe the movements of his host as he makes tea. If there are any questions, it is for the chief guest only to speak, since all verbal exchanges are conducted in a prescribed form, and anyone not familiar with those terms stands at the risk of sounding very odd. But after the *koicha* ceremony, the guests are at liberty to converse with one another or to smoke if they wish. But above all, proper dignity and good manners should be observed, and at no time should any- one talk or laugh excessively, which would disturb the atmosphere of the tea room.

When the tea utensils are presented for viewing, the guest, unless he is very experienced, should avoid touching the articles for fear of either damaging them or spilling the contents on the tatami floor. But it is up to the host to present his tea articles in such a way that the inexperienced guest will be given clues as to how to handle them properly.

Cakes

At all tea ceremonies, sweet cakes or *kashi* are served before the tea. Those made from sweet bean paste are called *namagashi* and are served with thick tea, while *higashi*, dry cookies with a sandy texture, are served with thin tea. At *koicha* gatherings, except for the very informal ones, it is usual for the special type of meal called *kaiseki* to be eaten before the sweets are served. After the guest has eaten the sweets, he goes out to rinse his mouth, thereby ensuring that the taste of the tea, which is drunk immediately afterward, is not spoiled.

These sweets are usually served on individual plates, the size of a saucer, and handled with a toothpick made of soft wood from the spice bush tree. The guest places the plate in front of his knees and transfers the cake to the thin tissue paper (*kaishi*) he brings with him, with the toothpick. The toothpick also serves as a knife to cut the sweets into bite-size pieces before eating. Sometimes, when the number of guests is uncertain, several pieces of cake are placed in a bowl (*hachi*) or lidded container (*futamono*). Since the *hachi* is rather large, about one foot in diameter, special chopsticks are provided to pick up the cakes.

It is also customary before eating to ask the permission of the other guests to eat first by saying, "*O saki ni*," or "Please excuse me for eating first." If the bowl containing the sweets is not placed straight in front of you, it should be moved until it faces you, then the thin tissue taken out and a piece of cake placed on it. Should the tips of the chopsticks become soiled in the process, they should be wiped first with the paper and then passed on to the next guest, but not before first admiring the bowl for a little while.

The lidded containers are used either to keep out the dust or to keep the sweets warm. Sometimes the layered container made of porcelain or lacquer, called *futa-mono* or *nurimono* respectively, is used to serve steamed cakes. In this case, it is for the chief guest to take the *kashi* in the bottom layer, the second guest to take from the next layer and so on. Chopsticks are provided to pick up the cakes and they are placed on the lid. The empty layers are passed back to the host.

Higashi are usually served in a tray or lacquered container and passed around.

98

It is usual, when there are two types of *higashi* in the tray, to take both, although not more than three pieces should be taken. The same procedure is repeated in this case, and before eating the *higashi* from the piece of thin tissue, you should excuse yourself for eating first.

How to Drink Tea

Usucha

The tea bowl can either be placed in front of the guest or may be placed in the room where the tea ceremony was prepared. In the latter case, when the bowl has to be brought from the other room, the guest has to go to the host to receive the tea. If the room is small, that is, less than four and a half mats, the guest should not stand up but advance on his knees toward the host. He should also remember the original place where the bowl was stored, so as to return it to its proper place after drinking the tea. The order for drinking tea when the tea bowl is placed before the guest could perhaps be clarified through a step-by-step procedure.

Place the tea bowl outside the border of the tatami you are sitting on. If there is a guest who has been served before you, it is polite to say, "*O shōban sasete itadaki masu*," or "Please let me accompany you." And to the guest who has not yet been served, you should excuse yourself for drinking first.

You then turn to the host and address him with the words, "*O temae o chōdai itashimasu*," or "I'll partake of your tea." When the tea has been prepared outside the room and brought in by someone else, then this address is unnecessary.

Pick up the bowl with your right hand and place it on the palm of your left hand. Put the fingers of your right hand around it, with the thumb facing you, and make a small bow as a sign of reverence.

With the bowl still resting on the palm of your left hand, grasp the rim of the bowl with your forefinger and thumb and turn it about ninety degrees clockwise.

Take a sip and then comment on how good it tastes, while dropping your right hand on the tatami before your knees.

Drink the remaining tea in small sips and when you come to the last sip, inhale deeply, making an audible sound and finish the tea.

After drinking, the rim of the bowl should be wiped lightly with tissue paper from left to right, as you hold the bowl between forefinger and thumb.

With the bowl still resting on your left palm, turn it counterclockwise so that it reverts to its original position before you drank from it. This is done with the thumb at the edge of the bowl and the other four fingers underneath it.

Place the bowl on the outside of the tatami border and, with your hands on the mat, gaze at the bowl to appreciate its shape. The bowl can be picked up with both hands to view it more closely, although in this case, it is not good manners to raise the bowl too high to admire it.

Pick up the bowl and return it to the original position or to the host. In this case the bowl should be turned twice in a 180 degrees revolution so that the front of the bowl faces your host when you return it to him.

Koicha

Koicha can be drunk with three or more guests together or even when you are the only guest. The tea can either be served by an attendant or the guest can go to fetch it himself, but in either case a *kobukusa*, or piece of brocade to rest the bowl on, is placed beside him.

The main guest places the bowl on the inside of the tatami border, to the left of the *kobukusa*, between himself and the second guest. The two then address each other with formal exchanges like, "Let us partake of the tea together."

The main guest places the *kobukusa* on his left palm and the tea bowl on top of it. If the brocade which he is presented with is very valuable, the guest will put it temporarily to the right of his knees and take out his own which he uses to rest the

100

bowl on. He then grasps the bowl with the thumb in front of him, and the other fingers on the opposite side of the bowl, and nods to the host to indicate that he is going to taste the tea.

He revolves the bowl ninety degrees clockwise, avoids touching the "face" of the bowl, and with the edge of the *kobukusa* pinched between the forefinger and middle finger of his right hand, he takes a sip of tea.

At this time the host will ask him about the taste of the tea, and the guest replies politely, and then takes two and a half sips of tea. It is now the turn of the next guest to drink, who precedes this move with a word of apology which is acknowledged by a slight bow.

After three and a half sips, the guest places the bowl, with the *kobukusa* underneath it, on the inside border of the tatami mat. He takes a thin tissue and wipes the rim of the bowl from left to right, then folds it in four and returns it to his kimono pocket. The bowl is then rotated to the original position, with two turns of ninety degrees each, and if done correctly the front of the bowl will face the next guest squarely.

He then passes the bowl to the next guest with the *kobukusa* underneath it. If the next guest is a member of the opposite sex, he will place the bowl on the inside border of the tatami between himself and the next guest, speaking some words of greeting as he does so. In this instance the two guests will turn to face each other momentarily, and return to their original positions after it is over. He will touch the tatami with his hands and make a bow, and a nod will be received as a sign of acknowledgment. These actions are called *okurirei* and *kaerirei* respectively.

The next guest repeats the actions of the first guest, although he does not nod to the host, for the tea should be drunk while it is hot.

When the second guest has taken one sip, the chief guest asks the host for the name of the tea he is serving and the district where it was grown.

When the last guest has finished the tea, indicated by a slight hissing sound, the main guest asks for the bowl in order to admire it. The bowl is wiped and brought to the main guest, who passes it around for proper inspection.

Hanging Scrolls, Flowers and Incense

A scroll, called *kakemono*, and flowers always accompany the tea ceremony. They are placed in the special alcove, or in the case where no alcove exists, they are hung on one section of the wall. Occasionally, a flower vase can also be hung from the wall.

The scroll is usually only shown in the earlier part of the tea ceremony, to be removed and replaced by flowers in the latter half. This arrangement makes it easier for the guests to appreciate the art and the flowers separately, and it also serves to change the atmosphere of the room, but in an evening tea ceremony, flowers can be displayed during the earlier part of the gathering as well.

When the guest arrives at the tea room, he goes directly to the alcove to examine the scroll before even greeting the host, since the host has taken considerable trouble in choosing a scroll which blends harmoniously with the season or the purpose of the occasion. When this is done, the guest goes to his seat, from where he greets his host, venturing some opinion on the beauty of the painting. He will also express his gratitude to his host for having taken such pains to entertain him.

The function of the *kakemono* is best expressed by a quote attributed to Rikyū, which says, "The most important tea utensil is the *kakemono*, for it is one aspect of *cha-no-yu* which both the host and the guest can appreciate fully."

There are primarily two types of hanging scrolls: calligraphy, of which there are several kinds, *bokuseki, kohitsu, shōsoku, gasan*; and paintings, which can be classified into *tōga, suiboku* or *nanga*. The word *bokuseki* itself means calligraphy, but in the tea ceremony it specifically refers to works done by Zen priests of the Sung and Yuan dynasties of China, although today the works of high priests of the Daitoku-ji in

Kyoto are also referred to as *bokuseki*. The contents of these scroll writings can either be poems expounding Buddhist canons, the teachings of famous masters or simply the names of famous disciples. The works are hung in the alcove to be appreciated and understood by the guest, and for this reason, they are the most valuable type of hanging scroll used today.

Between the tenth and thirteenth centuries, many excellent specimens of calligraphy were done, and they were later cut out and individually framed to hang in the alcove. These were known as *kohitsu*. As Japanese literature began to flourish during this period, even emperors, court nobles and women of letters produced very good calligraphy in the poems or songs they wrote. This type of scroll was first used by Jō-ō in 1553, and even today, whenever *kohitsu* are hung in tea rooms, the mood is instantly suggestive of the graceful elegance of the Heian period.

Letters written by men of virtue, distinguished by a very distinct style, were known as *shōsoku*, which may be either wholly or partly framed and mounted on a scroll. Sometimes a good painting would be inscribed with critical remarks from admirers, and these are known as *gasan*. They may be written by the painter himself, or they may be words of appreciation from several different people, usually expressed in the form of a poem.

The theme of the paintings hung in the alcove would usually be birds, flowers or landscapes, and during the Muromachi period, the most precious works were those done by the T'ang, Sung and Yuan painters in China. Perhaps the most valuable of all these were the works of a Chinese painter by the name of Hsiao Hsiang, whose "Eight Scenes" depicting the scenery around Lake Tungting in central China was not only greatly admired, but also influenced Japanese ink paintings in the succeeding years. Zen priests studied his art during their training period, and their works were subsequently found to be best suited to the peaceful and relaxed atmosphere of a tea house.

As a result of this preference for works of art, Japanese schools of painting multiplied during this period, and a specific Japanese style of art evolved with the appearance of many bright and brilliant compositions in blue and gold. These lavish works were hung in the waiting room alcove, since their brilliance clashed somewhat with the mystery of the ink paintings in the tea room alcove.

Since the scroll is an object for admiration in the tea room, it is always framed very thoughtfully. There are several styles, ranging from the simple to the intricate, depending on the type of materials used, and on whether it is a scroll painting or calligraphy. Most of the scrolls used in the tea room are mounted on paper, while the more lavish ones are mounted on gold brocade or patterned silk. The mounts vary in keeping with the design of the tea room or the fame of the artist or calligrapher. Usually simple mounts are used for paintings and gold brocade for calligraphy, although some poems may call for more lavish, patterned silk instead. But by far the most important rule for the hanging scroll in the alcove is to see that it matches the proportions of the alcove itself, for no matter how well mounted the scroll may be, if it does not balance with the measurements of the alcove, the effect will be discordant.

25. A sixteenth-century Ōido tea bowl named Kizaemon.

26–27. Two aspects of the Kizaemon tea bowl.

28. A sixteenth-century black Raku tea bowl named Tarō.

29. A seventeenth-century red Raku tea bowl named Jū-ō.

30–31. A late sixteenth-century yellow Seto bowl with floral
design (*top*), and a sixteenth-
century Oribe covered dish for
sweets (*bottom*).

32. A sixteenth-century tea caddy called Sōgo-nasu, and the caddy bag.

33. A bamboo tea scoop made by Rikyū.

34. A seventeenth-century incense case made in the form of a mandarin duck by Ninsei.

35. A sixteenth-century flower vase made in the Iga style.

36. A glazed hanging flower vase produced in the Echizen kilns.

37. This *shoin*-style tea room shows the alcove decorated with both hanging scroll and flower vase.

38. A specimen of brushwork written by a Chinese Zen priest.

39. The stand (*daisu*) and articles used for *shoin*-style tea ceremonies.

40. The simple alcove of the *sōan*-style tea room.

41. The utensils for a *sōan*-style tea ceremony using the firing pit.

115

42. A tea bowl containing powdered green tea which is the basis
of both *koicha* and *usucha*.

116

43. The portable brazier is used to heat the kettle in the summer months.

44. The most usual form of *temae* is when the host himself prepares the tea.

45. Smelling incense at the start of the tea ceremony.

46. A "guard" stone (*sekimori*) is placed in the garden to show guests the way.

47. One of the arbors in the gardens of the Katsura Imperial Villa, where guests wait before the tea ceremony.

48. The entrance to the tea room of the Shōkintei in the Katsura Imperial Villa.

120

49. The dome-shaped entrance to the tea room in the Shōkintei.

50. The tea room in the Shōkintei.

51. The preparation area of the Gepparō tea house in the Katsura Imperial Villa consists only of a pair of simple shelves and a cooking area.

52. This preparation area constructed in the mid-nineteenth century has since had gas and water facilities added to it.

53. Washing the hands and mouth just before the tea ceremony is a symbolic act of purification.

54. During an evening tea ceremony, the lanterns in the garden are lit and the hostess comes out to greet the guests with a candle.

55. The guests wait in the arbor until the gong signals them into the tea room.

56. The host waits in the preparation room while the guests eat
the *kaiseki* meal.

57. The *kaiseki* is brought out on a tray and handed to the guests.

58. Calligraphy is one of the arts which a tea master should acquire.

59. Tea masters usually carve their own tea scoops out of bamboo.

60. The ash in the portable brazier is first molded with an ash spoon before the charcoal is set alight.

61. In the preparations for making *usucha* using the portable brazier (plates 61–68), the tea ladle is handled according to form.

62. The tea scoop is carefully wiped with the silk cloth (*fukusa*) both at the start and end of *temae*.

63. The tea bowl is warmed with hot water and wiped dry with a white linen cloth before the tea is made.

64. The powdered green tea is scooped out of the special lacquered tea caddy and into the tea bowl.

128

66. Handling the ladle: after boiling water is poured into the bowl.

67. Handling the ladle: after the water is poured into the kettle.

65. Boiling water is added to the tea using the ladle, which must be correctly handled.

68. The ladle is placed on the rim of the kettle after its use.

69. Adding charcoal to the firing pit (plates 69–72) also conforms to a set procedure, beginning with the lifting of the kettle.

70. Wet ash is scattered over the already molded ash pattern in the firing pit.

71. The largest piece of charcoal is taken from the charcoal basket and placed into the firing pit by hand.

72. A smaller piece of round charcoal is then put over this with a pair of metal chopsticks.

131

73. Charcoal has to be cut very carefully with a sharp saw to prevent the edges from being ragged or uneven.

74. Preparations for making *koicha* (plates 74–79) differ from those of *usucha*, but they both start with the wiping of the tea caddy.

75. The silk material used to wipe the tea caddy (*fukusa*) is handled very carefully and according to proper convention.

76. The powdered tea is first scooped up and then poured into the tea bowl.

77. Boiling water is ladled into the tea bowl.

78. The mixture of powdered tea and boiling water is blended with the whisk.

79. When the tea is ready, the host offers the bowl to the first guest.

80. The host arranges the tea scoop, the tea caddy and its bag for the guests' appreciation after they have drunk the tea.

134

81. Before *koicha* is drunk, it is customary to eat some sweets (*kashi*).

82. When the guest has finished drinking, he wipes clean the area which his mouth has touched.

83. The bowl is passed on to the next guest according to proper etiquette.

84. A tea ceremony held outdoors, called *nodate*, is subtly influenced by the changing of the seasons.

136

PERFORMANCE OF
A TEA CEREMONY

A tea ceremony performance where up to five guests are invited at a time can roughly be divided into three sections, the preliminary part, the middle part and the final part.

In the first part, called the *zenseki*, the windows are curtained off by bamboo screens to darken the room, the scroll is removed, and a new one put in its place. In special dawn or dusk tea gatherings, a vase of flowers alone will decorate the alcove.

In the middle part of the ceremony, called the *nakadachi*, a very simple *kaiseki* meal is served, followed by sweet cakes, after which the guests retire for a moment of relaxation into the inner garden or *roji*.

During the final stage of the tea ceremony known as the *nochi-iri*, the scroll in the alcove is replaced by a floral arrangement, and the water jar, tea caddy and some of the tea utensils will be placed in the area where *temae* will be performed. The atmosphere of the room is quite changed from the *zenseki* period as the bright, burning charcoal lights up the entire room and fills it with a pleasant aroma. The host picks up the ladle, a signal for his assistant to roll up the bamboo screen brightening the room once again. The host performs *temae* in silence, while the guests concentrate on all his movements. This is the climax of the tea ceremony. The main guest will then speak, in the special formal language, to his host, while the other guests remain silent. Once the tea has been drunk and silence once more reigns, the fire is smothered by adding more charcoal to the fire pit and the sound of the boiling kettle subsides. Then thin tea is served, this being the sign that the tea ceremony is at an end.

On some occasions, after *koicha* has been drunk, the guests may be requested to move into another room where they are served with thin tea. Then the process of covering the flames does not take place. The whole event is characterized by great solemnity, expressed by the words, *"ichi go ichi e"* or "one chance in one's lifetime."

In keeping with the serious nature of the ceremony, it has also become customary to take a bath and change into clean clothes just before it, and to arrive up to twenty minutes before the ceremony takes place. Most tea ceremonies are held at noon, but depending on the season and the occasion, they may also be held at dawn, early morning, in between meals, in the late afternoon, in the evening, or at night. When an unexpected guest turns up, it can be performed at any hour.

It is the rule to invite the main guest first, and after consultation with him, the host selects the other guests. The host also inquires whether the time or date he has chosen for *cha-no-yu* is convenient for the main guest, a polite precaution to avoid unnecessary complications.

Preparations Made by the Host

THE TEA ROOM

Before a tea gathering, the host will make sure that the tea room is cleaned thoroughly and that the fire pit, the tatami mats, the linen tea cloth, the tea whisk, the ladle and *fukusa* are all spotless. The chopsticks, the lid rest, the water pipe leading to the wash basin, the chopsticks for the debris pit in the garden are all replaced by new ones made of green bamboo. And finally he will make sure that all the tea utensils necessary for the ceremony are arranged in their proper places, and the ceremony can start as soon as the guests arrive.

A small room near the gate in the garden is always provided for the guests to wait before the start of the ceremony. A carpet is laid out there for the guests to sit on, and cups of hot water are provided for the thirsty. An iron kettle is put above the stove (*hibachi*). A tobacco tray is placed inside the waiting room with a container for loose tobacco nearby, as well as two Japanese pipes (*kiseru*). There is also a charcoal fire in a small box surrounded by ash, beside which is a device known as *haifuki* used for blowing away ash from the tobacco. Smoking is not permitted in the tea room.

THE INNER GARDEN

The inner garden or *roji* is swept clean in the morning and the grass and shrubbery around the wash basin (*tsukubai*) are cut and trimmed. The inside and the bottom of the basin are washed and any stray stones around it swept away. A Japanese straw hat and wooden sandals (*geta*) are kept in case of rain. The garden is sprinkled with water, the amount usually varying according to the season. In winter, only the stepping stones, or *tobi-ishi*, and the lower portion of the bamboo fence are sprayed with water.

THE OUTSIDE WAITING AREA

The outside waiting area (*soto-machiai*) usually consists of a wooden bench with straw cushions and a tobacco tray. In cold weather a kind of heater, called *teaburi*, or the *hibachi*, is used to keep the guests warm, and a wooden pail of hot water is provided for the elderly to wash their hands and rinse their mouths.

THE PREPARATION ROOM

This room (*mizuya*) is also thoroughly cleaned and all the utensils needed to make the charcoal fire and to serve the two kinds of tea are put in their proper places before the beginning of *temae*.

THE MEAL

All the necessary utensils for the *kaiseki* meal, which include the lacquered tray or a low table, called *zen*, and the different types of bowls, plates and vessels, are prepared and kept ready. The tea ceremony can begin, as soon as all the guests are assembled and ready.

Various Types of Tea Ceremonies

THE NOON TEA CEREMONY

As this is the most formal of the different types of tea ceremonies, it serves as a good example to explain the different actions of the host and guests. During the fifteen minute stay in the waiting room, the guests study the hanging scroll, the floral decorations and change into clean white socks (*tabi*) in preparation for entering the tea room.

When all the guests have arrived, an attendant will guide them to the outside waiting area. The host, learning that everyone is present, goes out into the inner garden to rinse his mouth with water from the wash basin, carrying with him a wooden pail filled with water and the tea ladle. He scoops some water from the wash basin into the wooden pail and then pours all the contents of the pail into the basin, a signal to his guests that he has filled the basin. He replaces the ladle and wooden pail in their original place in the garden and goes toward the middle gate to welcome his guests.

When the guests hear the host opening the middle gate of the outer garden, they advance towards him, and both host and guests greet each other with a silent bow. The host then shuts the gate and returns to the tea room, leaving the door of the small guests' entrance (*nijiriguchi*) partially open.

The guests follow the host to the middle gate and walk in single file toward the wash basin to wash their hands, at the same time observing and admiring the garden and scenery.

The main guest then walks along the stepping stones toward the tea room, crouches on the stepping stone in front of the tiny entranceway, and slides the

140

partially open door to enter head-first, followed by the other guests. As he enters the room he leans his straw sandals (*zōri*) against the lower wall outside the entrance, and the others do the same. The last person to enter slides the door shut with a small bang and locks it with a clicking sound to tell the host that all are now assembled in the tea room. These preliminary rules are known as *seki-iri*, or rules for entering the tea room.

The host now comes out of his preparation room to welcome his guests verbally for the first time, although his greeting will only be directed toward the main guest, for it is considered proper for the other guests to remain silent. When this is over, the host goes back into the preparation room, brings out all the tea utensils, and starts the charcoal fire, a procedure known as *sumi-demae*.

As the fire begins to burn, the guests are served with *kaiseki* food, which usually takes thirty to forty minutes, during which time the fire grows hot enough for the host to start the preparations for *koicha*. The host demonstrates his skills in the arrangement of charcoal in the fire so that it burns just strongly enough to boil the water in the kettle at exactly the right time and temperature. (In summer, when the fire pit is not used, the host waits until the meal is over before he heats the portable brazier.)

The *kaiseki* meal is only a snack and not meant to satisfy one's appetite, since it is the tea which is the highlight of the ceremony. There is one ritual involved in the eating of the meal, called *sakazukigoto*, and that is the sharing of one sake cup between the host and his guests, which gives a feeling of fraternization to the whole occasion. (This often happens today at drinking parties.) In a formal tea gathering, the cup takes a zigzag course between the host and all his guests, but in other instances, the cup is only exchanged between the host and the main guest. This practice varies according to the type of guests present or the amount of time available for the ceremony.

When the meal is over, the guests replace all the bowls and dishes in their original positions, dropping their chopsticks on the tray with a sharp clicking sound. The host, who does not share the meal with his guests except to drink with them, will know that the meal is over and emerges from his seated position behind the host's entrance to the tea room to collect the trays. Everyone is silent during this interlude, and a sense of tranquillity pervades the room. The main guest must now concentrate on the actions of the host, for it is one of the aims of *cha-no-yu* to bring the feelings of host and guests into perfect harmony.

When all the guests are ready for the next part of the ceremony, the host places the pieces of charcoal in the portable brazier and arranges the ash in the brazier into the shape of a crescent moon, using a special spoon. This process may take up to forty minutes, for since the ash is only going to be used for the one occasion, any flaws or irregularities in the design means that the host must start all over again.

When the fire pit is used, the ash is rougher, and so a little water is first sprinkled on it to allow the air trapped at the bottom of the tray to circulate more freely.

The charcoal used to boil water is usually cut into uniform small pieces, the size depending on whether the fire pit or the brazier is used for *cha-no-yu*. It is the size of the charcoal pieces which determines the time it takes and the correct temperature, to boil the water.

THE DAWN CEREMONY (*Akatsuki no Chaji*)

This kind of ceremony is usually performed to bid a friend who is leaving early in the morning, farewell, and is most often held in winter when the fire pit is used. The first part of the ceremony is usually over before dawn, and the guests enter the tea room between three and four in the morning. (In earlier times this ceremony was known as *zantō no chaji* because the moon was still in the sky and the stone lanterns around the inner garden would still be alight.) The kettle is put over a charcoal fire started the previous evening, and the room is dimly-lit with candles in order to view the stone lanterns in the inner garden.

142

The guest is first offered some tea, which is followed by *shozumi*, when charcoal is placed in the fire pit; and then the *kaiseki* meal is eaten. In very cold weather, a few pieces of charcoal are taken out of the fire pit and placed in a container for the guests to warm their hands. A fresh kettle of water is brought and placed over the fire pit. A host has to be very experienced in order to hold an early morning ceremony, while the guest has to be equally experienced in order to fully appreciate it.

THE EVENING CEREMONY (*Yobanashi no Chaji*)
This type of ceremony is held on long wintry nights, usually preceded by leisurely conversation between the host and guests. Tea is first served, followed by the making of the charcoal fire, and the *kaiseki* meal is then eaten. After the thick tea and thin tea are drunk, there is another ceremony performed for lighting the fire, called *tatezumi*, during which the host continues to talk with his guests while listening to the pleasant crackle of charcoal. It is normal, on these occasions, to light the room with lanterns made of wood and paper, and because of this, flowers are not used to decorate the alcove, since the light distorts their natural colors. There are occasions, if the season is right, when white plum blossoms or white narcissus are displayed.

THE EARLY MORNING CEREMONY (*Asa-cha*)
This is only held in the summer months, usually between five and six in the morning to avoid the heat of the sun. The host moves rather quickly throughout the ceremony and the entertainment ends rapidly.

MEALTIME CEREMONY (*Hango no Chaji*)
This can either be held before or after meals, and only sweets, rather than *kaiseki*, is served. The sweets eaten during this type of ceremony are very special and include cakes made of glutinous rice. After the sweets, a bowl of clear soup will be drunk

and a cup of sake passed around and drunk in the usual fashion. Before *koicha* is served, the guests retire to the waiting room to wash their hands and relax. This is a contracted form of the formal tea ceremony, the biggest difference between the two being that only sweets and not the simple *kaiseki* meal are eaten before the drinking of tea. The ceremony also takes place rather hurriedly, and there is no lingering over the sweets.

SPECIAL TEA CEREMONY (*Atomi no Chaji*)
This is usually held for distinguished visitors when the host uses his most prized utensils. On occasions, art dealers or businessmen may ask to be allowed to attend in order to view the tea articles, and if they are granted permission, they must wait in a separate room, where they are served with sweets and thick tea, until the end of the ceremony to inspect the utensils.

IMPROMPTU CEREMONY (*Rinji no Cha-no-yu*)
This is usually held spontaneously, during auspicious moments such as viewing a full moon, the snow, cherry trees in bloom, or when a friend arrives unexpectedly from distant lands. Since the gathering is held without prior notice, it is not necessary for everything to be orderly. The floor is quickly swept and a kettle is placed over the fire pit or brazier, the guest is informally invited into the room and greetings are exchanged with the host. A simple meal of rice balls or rice covered with seaweed is speedily prepared and served on ordinary plates, and the tea utensils are not elaborate or numerous. However, one or two valuable utensils, perhaps the tea caddy or scroll, are shown to the guest, but it is generally rather informal.

Apart from the types of tea ceremonies mentioned above, there are other ceremonies which can be held for the cold season, the hot summer, New Year's Eve (*joya*), felicitations (*shūgi*), memorial services (*tsuizen*) and partings. There is also the rather unique *zanka* ceremony, where only distinguished citizens gather to watch a *wabi* master perform *cha-no-yu*, but in general the differences among them are very slight.

Flowers in the Tea Ceremony

The special floral arrangement used for tea ceremonies called *chabana* differs distinctly from *ikebana*, the traditional Japanese art of flower arrangement. *Chabana* has its roots in the earliest type of formal flower arrangement known as *rikka*, which is still used in large tea ceremonies held today, but it is not typical of *chabana*. In the early days of the tea ceremony it was normal to arrange flowers in an artificial, stilted style. Later on, the process was simplified and the old rules were ignored in favor of a new, less formal style, where the flowers were admired for their own beauty rather than for the method of arrangement.

As the tea ceremony progressed, the host performed *chabana* in front of the guests, and the techniques of arrangement gave way to placing flowers in a vase in the most natural way. (*Ikebana* uses the term *ikeru* meaning to arrange, while chabana uses *ireru* meaning to let in.) This also meant that only seasonal flowers would be used.

It was Rikyū who once said, "Arrange the flowers as you would find them in the fields," and his maxim is still followed by tea masters today. The flower vase is called *hana-ire*, which means a container in which flowers are placed, rather than *hana-ike*, used in *ikebana*, which means a container where flowers are arranged.

Other differences between *chabana* and *ikebana* may help to explain the philosophy behind the use of flowers in the tea ceremony. For instance, *ikebana* places sole importance on an artificial arrangement to express natural themes, but in *chabana* flowers are arranged without any artifice and put simply in a vase in their natural state. Since ancient times, *ikebana* has tried to express heaven, earth and the universe through its arrangements (although today it also expresses themes from nature), but the emphasis in *chabana* is placed on flowers in their growing state.

In *ikebana* the petals are sometimes plucked off to expose only the stamen and the pistil, or leaves and branches may be colored artificially, which is forbidden in *chabana*. Neither can wood, metal or stone be used to decorate the creation. Furthermore, flowers which are highly scented are never used in *chabana*, like the sweet smelling daphne (*skimmia japonica*), the cockscomb (*patrinia scabiosaefolia*), the pomegranate, the pond lily (*nuphar japonicum*), or pot marigold (*calendula officinalis*).

In former times seasonal changes were emphasized in *ikebana*, but modern greenhouses and rapid airfreight has put an end to that principle. Nowadays, practically all kinds of flowers can be found at a florist, regardless of the season, and for this reason, the seasonal theme has lost its importance in the art.

On the other hand, the rules of *chabana* are more rigid, and ideally, only flowers which appear early in the season are used in the tea room. Flowers in the garden or those picked in mountains or fields are the best types to use, and those which have been cultivated artificially are strictly forbidden by tea masters. The ancient masters used to say that *chabana* should be arranged "with one's feet," which meant only the flowers cultivated in one's garden were considered suitable.

In *chabana*, the flowers are only used for the duration of the ceremony—that is, about an hour—and as soon as they have played their part in the ceremony, they are discarded, unlike *ikebana*, where the flowers are kept for a week or so. Thus flowers which are too sturdy or too gaudy are never displayed in the alcove.

Ikebana and *Chabana*
THE DIFFERENCE BETWEEN ARRANGING AND PLACING
It usually takes a long time to arrange the flowers for *ikebana*, but an experienced person is supposed to arrange *chabana* in just a few minutes, while the flowers are still fresh. Too long a time spent on *chabana* might cause them to wilt

146

and the decision as to which flowers to pluck and which container to place them in is made before the guests arrive.

The tea master will cut off all the unnecessary leaves and branches from the flowers, perhaps adding a twig for special effect. He then picks up all those he has selected and places them in the vase, making only a few minor adjustments in the way they fall. Only a seasoned tea master is able to accomplish what may seem a simple procedure both quickly and beautifully.

In *chabana* it is considered improper to use scissors or tools of any kind, and usually the master breaks off the stem with his hands. The art of flower arrangement allows the use of wires or special holders with needles sticking from them to help in its creation.

Ikebana also permits the use of several different types of flowers in one vase, or a bunch of the same flower may be arranged together, while in *chabana* only one flower is normally used, sometimes two, depending on the size of the flower as well as that of the container. In this case, it is only one flower which plays a dominant role; the other acts as a prop and is either half-open or still a bud.

This rule was also originated by Rikyū, who advised the use of as few flowers as possible. "Flowers arranged in a small room should be single in number, or at the most, two," is still heeded by tea masters today. This allows for the appreciation of only one species at a time, and for this reason, all obscuring leaves and twigs must be removed beforehand.

In *chabana* the flower vase itself is an object of appreciation. For instance, when a bamboo container is used, great care is taken that the cut surfaces along the front are not hidden from view. If a woven basket is used, then the handle is left unobscured, so large blooms are generally avoided because they detract from the vessel's appearance. In *ikebana*, on the other hand, the vessel does not play such an important part, since the stress is more on the flowers themselves.

There are four different locations in the tea room where the flower vase can be placed: on the tatami mat in the alcove, hung on the alcove wall, hung on the alcove pillar, or hung from the alcove ceiling.

The first instance, when the flower vase is placed in the alcove beside the pillar facing the guest, derived from the ancient custom of placing an incense burner in the center of the alcove in front of the Buddha figure or Buddhist scroll. The candlestand was put on the right and the flowers on the left of the figure or painting. Sometimes when the alcove was planned in reverse order, the flower container would naturally be placed on the right. Usually a thin board is put between the tatami and the vase, but if the alcove is not covered with tatami, no boards are necessary. If the scroll is very wide, the vase can be put in the center of the alcove. In a very small tea room the vase is hung in the center of the alcove wall. A nail is driven in when the scroll is removed, and the vase is hung usually about three feet or so from the ground.

When both flowers and scroll are displayed at the same time, a bent nail is driven into the side of the pillar facing the guests' entrance.

Sometimes a special boat-shaped container is used (*tsurifune*), originally imported from China and made of metal, but now produced domestically and made from either bamboo or pottery. The front of the container is directed toward the room, and the whole arrangement is suspended from the center of the alcove ceiling.

Another important rule to follow, apart from those mentioned earlier, is to balance the flowers with the vase. Usually the flowers are not larger in diameter than the mouth of the container, and they are never taller than the container. When the flowers have been placed in the vase, water is then sprinkled over them.

INCENSE

The first smell to greet you when you enter a tea room is the strong sweet aroma of incense which masks the smell of charcoal. The type known as *kōboku* is used with the brazier, another one, *nerikō*, is used with the fire pit. There are two different ways of burning incense, either directly in the fire (*shokō*), or placed near the fire and burned slowly (*kinkō*). Sometimes the incense is separated from the fire by a thin piece of mica. This procedure is known as *chūkō*, and is only used on very special occasions. There are also two types of incense burners, one called *kōro*, used to perfume the entire room, and a small one called *kikigōro*, which is usually picked up by the guests for a fragrant whiff.

TEA ARCHITECTURE
AND TEA GARDENS

Since earliest times all sorts of rooms have been used for tea-drinking: from the splendid *shoin* (reception room) to the *sōan* (hut) room. After many changes, the *sōan* room was finally selected as the most suitable place to enjoy tea without distraction.

There are, however, four different styles of tea architecture: the large drawing room, the hut which expressed the merchant's taste, the room that appealed to the samurai class, and the aristocrat's tea pavilion. It may be felt that only the *sōan* is a true tea room, but it is important to know the background of each of the four types in order to understand the evolution of *cha-no-yu*. Since gardens also reflect the aesthetics of tea, their origins and features in relation to the tea ceremony are also examined.

From *Shoin* to *Sōan*

Before the Heian era, most Japanese architecture was in the Shinden style, a design adopted for the building of temples, shrines, and nobles' residences. In the course of time a new samurai-style dwelling was introduced, and later, in the Muromachi era, the *shoin* style was conceived.

Shoin originally meant a writing room or study found within a temple, usually a small wing attached to the drawing room. During the height of samurai power it was used as a living room or salon where guests were received. The floor was covered with tatami mats, and the room was equiped with an alcove and a few ornamental shelves.

There were various ways of arranging the alcove and shelves, but the most popular one was to have the *shoin* window desk (*tsuke-shoin*) face the veranda, and next to it, the alcove and shelves were placed side by side. Since there was no artificial lighting available in those days, the *shoin* desk had to be built near the window, and the alcove was situated beside it. Even today this is a basic rule followed in designing Japanese-style drawing rooms.

In the years before the *shoin* style was introduced, six-foot-long shelves called *taji*, built in the room adjoining the drawing room, were used for preparing tea. Some of them were built into the wall, while others were smaller in size and could be removed.

In the *shoin* room this procedure of using the *taji* area for *temae* was preserved. The room next to the *shoin* was called *kusari-no-ma* (the chain room), so named because it had a fireplace set into the floor, over which a kettle was suspended by chains from the ceiling. Tea was made in a separate room and then offered to the guests in the reception room.

Some time later, when the ritual of making tea came to be performed before the guests, shelves and vessels which were appropriate for the purpose were selected. Such shelves were used in earlier times when *temae* was carried out by the *dōbōshū* or menservants, and also on occasions when the nobles sat on the matted platform to watch *temae*. Thus they had to be presentable.

The *shoin* were opulent tea buildings, most of them as large as thirty-six tatami mats (162 sq. yds.), and for that reason they lacked the atmosphere that was conducive to proper composure of mind. It soon became the fashion to close off part of the room with a screen, which was known as a *kakoi* (enclosure). In later days the *kakoi* played an essential role in the *shoin* tea ceremony, and this design was incorporated into the special buildings for tea ceremonies.

In the Muromachi era houses were constructed with pillars set every seven feet. Tea houses, however, did not follow this rule, and their pillars were erected every three feet. This design enabled the construction of small houses of four and a half or six mats, like the Dōjin-sai tea room which Ashikaga Yoshimasa completed in Higashiyama, Kyoto, in 1486.

The tea master Shukō, who originated the idea of the host serving tea himself, designed an especially intimate tea room, whose walls and ceiling were similar to those of the *shoin*, but on a smaller scale. In that room Shukō placed a *daisu* (tea cabinet) where he performed *temae*. The ceremony held in a large room was meant to be observed by people, while Shukō's tea ceremony was meant to induce a congenial feeling between the host and guests.

The above-mentioned style of tea room, which was actually a small-style *shoin*, continued to be constructed until the late Muromachi era. It generally had a four-and-a-half-mat room, with a ceiling covered with thin overlapping boards called *noneita*, and papered walls. A small change was made in the late sixteenth century.

According to illustrations of Jō-ō's room in the *Record of Yamanoue Sōji*, the tea room is four and a half mats in size, and opens out onto the garden, which is situated in a northerly direction. A fire pit is built in the center of the floor. Three sides of the room are walls, while on the northern side there is a paper sliding door that faces a veranda. The wall on the eastern side separates the tea room from the *shoin*. This kind of tea room is typical of the rooms of that era, and there is written evidence to show that most people in Sakai imitated this style.

The drawing room of the house was designed to face east and south, in order to admit direct light. In contrast, the tea room was built to face north, for it was felt that a more subdued lighting would allow the mind to concentrate on the ceremony. Probably for the same reason today an artist's studio also admits light from the north, for the light from this direction is felt to have the most aesthetic effect on tea articles and on paintings.

The fire pit used in the tea room was, on the average, a bit less than one and a half feet square. In earlier days a charcoal or wood-burning hearth was set in the living room or the room adjoining the drawing room, but was never used for guests. It was bigger, sometimes as large as a tatami mat, and was built into the same part of the tatami as the portable brazier was placed in the warm season. Later the fire pit was positioned between host and guests, at the most convenient place for the host, who sat obliquely facing the guests to serve tea.

In building the fire pit, the pit is first made with boards, the inside of the pit is coated with mud, and it is then sunk into the flooring by cutting away part of the tatami, and a wooden cover is placed over it.

The Characteristics of *Sōan*

In 1573 a great many castles were constructed for and by military generals. Nobunaga's Azuchi Castle was typical of these, and its architecture combined elements of a residence and a fortress. Such buildings were large and splendid, and their interiors were purposely lavish in order to display the rulers' power. Kanō Eitoku (1543–90) and his family were the creators of the wall paintings in these castles, as well as the beautiful paintings and screens found in many of Kyoto's temples. It was during this time that Kanō originated *koi-e*, a technique in which bright colors were painted over a gold background. In describing the effect of such paintings, G. B. Sansom in his book *Japan: A Short Cultural History* says:

> On the walls, mostly of bright gold, there are blue-eyed tigers prowling through groves of bamboo, or multi-colored *shishi*—mythical beasts like lions, but amiable and curly-haired—that gambol among peonies against a golden background. . . . As a rule these apartments display, suite after suite, such profusion of color and detail, such a deliberate effort to overwhelm the eye with splendor, that they come perilously near to vulgarity. But from this danger they are generally saved by a certain bravery, a boldness of stroke and brilliance of design.

In contrast with the samurai, the *machi-shū* of Sakai were wealthy enough to build whatever splendid buildings they chose, but they preferred simplicity. They chose tea rooms which had no gaudy decorations, required no artificial elements in their construction, and did not need an abundance of furniture. They influenced the change in style of the tea room and finally invented the simple *sōan* hut (called *kozashiki* in those days), using the natural materials of farmhouses: mud, straw, logs and rough wood. The *sōan* was based on a simple log structure typical of Japanese carpentry, but there was freedom to use any building material that had natural charm. It was built facing south, for light could be screened off by constructing deeper eaves. The *sōan* stripped away many aspects of Jō-ō's traditional-style tea hut, as well as most of the elements of the *shoin*-style structure. Its floor, ceiling and window took on new forms that were different from the earlier ones. This type of tea house was conceived to suit the needs of the times, when members of all classes met in a small hut.

Among the various changes in tea architecture brought about by the invention of the *sōan*-style tea house, the following are the most essential.

THE FLOOR

Until this period the drawing room always contained a raised platform where the higher-ranking people would sit. In the *sōan*, where all people were treated equally, there was a raised floor only in the alcove. The alcove was decorated with celebrated tea articles of ancient origin, for the raised platform indicated a more honorable seat than that for the other participants, who sat on the tatami mat at a lower level.

In this way, by displaying only valuable art pieces in the alcove, people from varying backgrounds could sit together on the floor. The Japanese still treat the alcove not only as an ornamental shelf, but also as a seat of honor, and this can be traced back to the tea ceremony room.

154

THE CEILING

The houses were built with high ceilings, but it was found that height in a small tea room did make the guests feel more restful. Even as early as Jō-ō's time the tea room's ceiling was reduced to seven feet, and in Rikyū's days it was less than six feet. In order to avoid a cramped feeling, the ceiling had alternating heights. For example, the alcove ceiling was made a little higher than the ceiling in other parts of the room and was covered with a piece of board, while the ceiling above the host's seat was made a little lower than the section above the guests' place in order to show his humility.

There was also a special ceiling which was formed by the naturally sloping roof, called *keshōyaneura tenjō* or *kakekomi tenjō*. This slanting ceiling made the room seem larger than it really was.

The lightweight materials used for tea room ceilings were shingles, wickerwork, bamboo and reeds, quite different from the finely worked boards used for the fretwork ceilings of the large *shoin* rooms.

THE WALLS

Paper walls evolved into mud walls when the builders began to use logs as supporting posts. At first the alcove walls were made of paper, but they too were soon constructed of mud, probably because these warm and softly textured walls were aesthetically in keeping with the dark interior of the tea room.

The use of mud for walls made it possible to create rooms with rounded corners, and for tea rooms to be built in a circular shape around a central post, neither of which could have been accomplished by using paper walls.

THE WINDOWS

The windows of the tea room were closely related to the construction of the walls. Before the *sōan* style was invented, a lintel, called *shiki kamoi*, was laid from one post to another, and the space between them was made into a window. This conven-

155

tional method was not suitable for letting light into the small tea hut, and the lintel also looked awkward and out of place. The *shitaji mado*, a window cut into the lower area of the wall could be built in various sizes and allowed more light in. This design was copied from farmhouse windows built since early times. Such low windows provided ventilation and a better view of the garden or natural scenery, since people sat on the floor.

Another characteristic of the tea hut window was the bamboo grilles, which not only let in more light, but helped to create a mood conducive to serenity of mind.

THE HOST'S ENTRANCE (*Sadōguchi*)
This is a miniature entrance used by the host, originally lower than it is today (five feet seven inches), through which the host has to crouch to enter—another device to instill a sense of humility in the host.

THE GUESTS' ENTRANCE (*Nijiriguchi*)
This is a second entrance, through which guests have to stoop to enter the tea room. It is said that in Jō-ō's time one had to enter the tea room on hands and knees from the veranda. An old illustration still in existence shows this entrance with a half-rolled bamboo screen outside its paper door, but today the entrance is made of wood.

The guests' crouched entrance signified humility, but also, as the room became smaller and it was necessary to stoop at the entrance to look at the hanging scroll inside, it also showed respect to the other guests already seated in the room.

When the *sōan* came into use, its entrance was so low that one had to crawl into the room. It is said that the old storm door of the main house was used as the sliding door for the *nijiriguchi*; this is evident from the position of its *san* (cross-piece). The door itself was made of three boards, one narrower than the other two, indicating that a newer board had been added to the other two.

There is one opinion which states that, because the *sōan* was built from the old timbers of the main house, all kinds of wood were used in its construction. The door of the *nijiriguchi* was perhaps added as a finishing touch. Therefore two different kinds of wood were always used in order to represent the fact that the house was made of waste timber. Although the truth of this idea is uncertain, the idea of using waste material to build the door and then adding a piece of straight-grained or first-quality board is logical in terms of the contrasting effect.

The tracks for the door of the *nijiriguchi* are made of two boards with a groove between them for rain to flow through. This is known as *hasami shikii* and is also employed in the storm doors of residences, but it is uncertain if the style of the *nijiriguchi* door is simply used to keep rain out. If so, all the other doors of the tea hut facing the outside would be made in a similar way, which they are not. Furthermore, the eaves of the *nijiriguchi* are deep enough to protect it from the rain. Therefore, the door's design must have some other purpose.

Some people say that the *nijiriguchi* is designed in such a way as to prevent the entrance of intruders, but this too is doubtful because the door is only a quarter of an inch thick and can easily be broken with a push. The bamboo grilles are fixed only with nails, so that they are easily replaceable each year. The window itself is fragile in structure, covered only by a sliding paper door, and the wall surrounding it is only a little more than one inch thick.

The *hasami shikii* (door tracks) are cleaned, for the host takes off the door in order to wash and wipe it before the guests arrive. When the guest crouches on the stepping stone and touches the door, he finds it still wet in places, which gives him a refreshing feeling. The door is left slightly ajar, so that he can open it with ease. The moment he opens it, the alcove and hanging scroll come into view. From this vantage point, he can see the interior of the small room. After a quick glimpse, he bends over and creeps in, head first. As a result of his difficult entry, he is made more conscious of the fact that he is in the tea room.

The last guest to enter shuts and latches the door. This door latch is made so simply that it does not guard the room against danger, but it gives the guests a feeling of isolation. Perhaps the purpose of building the *nijiriguchi* is to make those who pass through it realize that they are entering another world.

SOME OTHER ELEMENTS

The other features in the tea room—pillars, lintels, frames, ledges—are made as light and fragile as possible. Much care is taken to provide an aesthetic balance between their height and width. The *akari shōji*, a sliding paper-covered screen with a wooden frame and lattice, is used for letting in light as well as protecting guests from the cold wind. Opaque white paper of varying widths is pasted on the frame, and in tea rooms, thin seams must appear between the lattices.

In Rikyū's time there was a discussion about the proper width of the seam. When Rikyū was asked about this, he said: "One *bu* (one-eighth of an inch) is too narrow, but one-and-a-half *bu* is too wide." It seems that this answer did not give the exact measure, but by showing the maximum and minimum, Rikyū taught that the width should be decided according to the size of the room. This episode shows how precise Rikyū was, even concerning such minute details.

The introduction of the *sōan* had various influences on the method of serving tea and the use of tea utensils. Up to that time, a cabinet was used in the four-and-a-half mat tea room, but because the *sōan* was too small to accommodate one, the cabinet had to be eliminated. As a result, people enjoyed tea without adherence to traditional customs concerning the method of using tea articles, which helped to enhance the popularity of the tea ceremony.

Changes in the Tea Room

In Matsuya's *Record of Tea Ceremonies*, it is stated that during the decade after 1590 (Rikyū's last year), Matsuya Hisamasa rebuilt his tea hut five times, an indication of the changes in tea hut fashion. Following the appearance of the four-and-a-half-mat tea hut, other types with four mats, three mats, and two mats were devised. One mat or half a mat was the unit of measurement for these tea huts, which meant that the rooms were either square or rectangular in shape, and lacked variation.

Later on, the *daime* tatami was devised, which was about one foot five inches shorter than the regular mat, for with the disappearance of the tea cabinet, less space was required in the *sōan*. As a result of this new type of tatami, the style of the ceiling was changed to suit the shape of the room.

At the same time, the fire pit was placed between the host and guests, and the *nakabashira* (central post) was built close to it. An extended wall (*sode kabe*) was attached to the post, and a shelf was fixed to its side. This post, like the *daikoku-bashira* (farmhouse kitchen post), produced the effect of being the center of the tea room.

The above changes were made during Rikyū's lifetime. After his death, daimyo tea devotees such as Furuta Oribe and Kobori Enshū exerted their influence on the design of the tea room. They changed the *sōan* into a more refined room in order to suit the warriors' taste and, most conspicuously, altered the use of light in the tea hut. Oribe preferred a bright tea hut to the dimness which Rikyū felt would soothe the mind, and Enshū carried out Oribe's preference through his use of the skylight or *tsukiage mado*. In Enshū's tea house in Fushimi, skylights were built in three different places, including one above the place where *temae* was carried out, and eight windows were constructed at various levels along the walls. Altogether there were eleven light sources.

The treatment of guests was changed by daimyo tea masters. Oribe's tea room had a *shōbanseki* (seat for minor guests), which was a one-mat area situated behind a paper screen outside the tea room. Nobles and their followers were to sit separately, and a new etiquette was introduced to segregate the ranks.

159

Until this time the *nijiriguchi* (guests' entrance) had been built on either the left or right side of the facade, but Oribe and Enshū placed it in the center in order to separate the principal guest from lesser ones. For a similar reason, an entrance combining the host's entrance and the nobles' entrance was constructed and the principle of social equality in the tea room disappeared.

After this time the convention of placing the host's seat at a lower level than the guests was no longer observed, the ceiling above the host's place was no longer lowered, and the host's special alcove (*teishu doko*) was constructed instead. In the style originated by Oda Uraku and Katagiri Sekishū, the host performed *temae* in front of the alcove, especially when he served people of lesser rank, or in order to better display a favorite scroll hanging in the alcove. The Jikō-in tea room in Yamato (Nara Prefecture), constructed by Sekishū, is representative of this style.

Enshū also devised the formula of placing the host's seat and the alcove side by side, like a stage. Such an arrangement suited tea ceremonies performed by a daimyo or his *sadō* (chief tea master who served the daimyo), and it was also an effective room design.

The *sōan* was a tea hut with none of the *shoin* elements included in its design, but these were reintroduced by Enshū. Gradually the tea hut developed into a *shoin* tea room, because one of its functions was to serve as a reception room for visiting nobility. The *shoin* was often constructed next to the drawing room so that it would be easily accessible to guests, while the *sōan* was separated from the main building.

The *shoin* room had paper walls and *nageshi* (wooden lintels), and its sliding door frames were coated with black lacquer. Ornamental shelves and a *shoin* desk were added to its design. Furthermore, although it had a *nijiriguchi*, the guests were able to enter through a veranda, rather than having to pass through the garden in sandals. It is said that this change came about to save the trouble of placing sandals on the ground for oneself, for part of the etiquette of tea was for guests to rest

160

their sandals in an upright position against the stepping stone before entering the room.

Such *sōan* elements as the *daime* (small-sized) tatami and *nakabashira* (center post) were retained in *shoin* architecture, but many other elements, as well as the philosophy of tea, were changed. However, there were also tea devotees who wished to preserve the *wabi* elements.

During the same epoch, Sōtan was a noted tea master, but unlike Rikyū, he did not give instruction to warriors and court nobles and clung tenaciously to the *wabi* tea style. He preserved the formalities of the Rikyū tea room, and his style was followed by the *machi-shū* of Sakai.

Kanamori Sōwa was a tea master descended from samurai stock, and had access to court nobles, whom he guided in both the tea ceremony and tea architecture. He had great influence on the design of temples and nobles' residences, and preferred the *sōan* to the *shoin* style, because he found restfulness in its small space. In contrast with Sōtan's tastes, Sōwa also wished to impart a sense of elegance to the tea ceremony.

Thus *wabi* and daimyo styles of tea coexisted to some extent, beginning with 1585 when Hideyoshi served tea at the Imperial Palace with Rikyū as his *sadō*. This event established the aristocratic tea ceremony, which incorporated Rikyū's *wabi* style in its fundamental concept.

Prince Toshihito, a member of the first generation of the Katsuranomiya family, constructed *shoin-sukiya* (a *wabi*-style tea hut characterized by a sense of irregularity and naturalness) tea houses on the premises of his palace in 1602, and sixteen years later added a two-mat tea room and a *kusari-no-ma* (chain room). The Katsura Imperial Villa, which was founded a little later, also included independent tea houses. The ex-emperor Gomino-o (1596–1680), who was well versed in the tea ceremony, built these tea rooms in his palace and in some temples.

What is most striking in these tea buildings is the aristocratic taste for extravagance, expressed in motifs representative of the upper class, such as the exquisitely shaped catches of sliding doors, the artistic design on the lower part of the *shōji* (paper screens) and the elaborate patterns on shelves. The pine, bamboo and plum designs which decorate the host's entrance to the Tōshin-tei tea room are fine examples of this cultured taste.

Simultaneously, there was a similar trend among commoners to make the structure of the *sōan* more intricate. This influence can be seen in the *itadatami* (a board which was added to the tea room in order to enlarge the space), or in the idea of designing the alcove on a smaller scale. Most people sought to display their originality in minor details, but at the same time it became the fashion to use expensive timber to make the house more elaborate. Thus the conventional, simple tea house that had symbolized the spirit of tea gradually came to possess more decorative elements.

In the Meiji era, when Western-style architecture was introduced into Japan, a blend of Japanese and European styles was adopted for ordinary homes, and typical Japanese buildings became scarce. In keeping with this tendency, orthodox tea houses and elegant tea huts disappeared, and the only buildings that resembled tea houses were those built on the grounds of restaurants and inns.

Tea Houses of Today

In early times, the *sōan* was generally made from natural materials found in one's surroundings, or from the old timbers of the main house. Through studying old tea structures that have been preserved, we can see that they were usually built of several kinds of timber, while in residential homes only one kind of wood (cypress or cedar) was used.

Tea houses built today follow ancient design in the choice of materials. However, it is now difficult to obtain materials that used to be available in earlier times,

162

and there are few carpenters who are able to build these tea houses, for the art of using logs combined with the skill of making mud walls have become rare and specialized.

In early times tea houses could easily be renovated according to taste, but today it is too expensive to change the structure once it has been built. This may also be due to present methods of construction. One of the basic principles in former tea architecture was lightness, where it was unnecessary to lay a foundation, as was the case for residential homes. Instead, a tea house pillar was set on a stone about eight inches in diameter, but now the beams and eaves of the tea house have become larger and heavier, since they are constructed by modern methods. They also require firm foundations of concrete, and the result is a permanent, solid, heavy appearance. They can hardly be called *sōan* in the true sense of the word.

Recently even a pre-fabricated tea house was put on the market and although it offers everyone an opportunity to own a tea house, this has the danger of making all tea houses uniform in appearance. The tea house should be designed not only in accordance with the size of its garden, but also to take into account the view of its roof from the main house. In a similar manner, windows are designed on the basis of the amount and quality of light they admit, as well as the view they command. The modern tea house today lacks the warmth, softness and comfort of the individually designed tea hut, and unfortunately the art and skill of earlier artisans is rarely found today. Houses styled naturally and without artifice differ greatly from those produced through modern techniques of imitation. Nevertheless, tea room characteristics such as lightness, asymmetry, and the use of natural woods and hidden posts are still preserved in some examples of contemporary Japanese architecture.

The Origin of Tea Gardens

The garden surrounding the tea house differs from the one outside the drawing room: the former is designed so the viewer may enjoy the scenery as he walks counterclockwise along the path around the pond, while the latter may be viewed from a seated position within the house.

According to the records of tea gatherings during the Muromachi period, the garden played an important part in tea entertainment, for after the banquet the guests went out to the garden to rest in the cool air near the pond, and then into a pavilion to have tea. A quiet place in the garden away from the main house was felt to be most suitable for drinking tea, and the participants felt more relaxed after going into the garden for a walk. One of such tea pavilions still in existence today is the Ginkaku-ji in Kyoto.

An illustration of Jō-ō's garden around his four-and-a-half-mat tea hut, found in the *Record of Yamanoue Sōji*, depicts two gardens, the *waki-no-tsubonouchi* (outer section close to the garden entrance) and the *omote-tsubonouchi* (the inner section near the tea hut).

In another illustration of a garden designed for the same type of tea hut by Ikenaga Sōsaku, Jō-ō's pupil, the *omote-tsubonouchi* is called *niwa* (garden) and the *waki-no-tsubonouchi* is called the inner garden. It is apparent from these terms that there was some difference in function between the outer garden and the inner garden, the latter being merely a passageway leading to the tea hut. The same picture shows that the inner garden had an entrance from which a five-foot-long path led to the the veranda adjoining the reception room.

A tea book written at the time, *Senrin*, stated that the garden in front of a four-and-a-half-mat tea hut should not contain any plants or stones, lest the guests be distracted by the scenic view, although it was permissible to have some greenery around the stone wash basin. It seems that this prohibition lasted for some time; a plan of the tea hut built by Matsuya Hisamasa in 1587 shows that the garden was laid out very simply, devoid of any plants, except for some moss and one maple tree.

Although Jō-ō's garden contained no trees, it undoubtedly had a lovely atmosphere. A book written at the time states that pines of various shapes could be seen overhanging the fence of his garden and provided a fine view in contrast to the garden's starkness.

Later on, when all four sides of the tea houses were walled, and the door of the guests' entrance was constructed of wood, there was no fear that they would be distracted by the outside view. As a result, the garden came to be designed with trees and shurbs, and stepping stones enabled the guests to walk around the garden with ease.

The *roji* (inner tea garden) came into existence because townspeople living along a crowded street sought its quietude and were able to stroll leisurely around the pond, even though it was merely a short distance from the city's hustle and bustle.

The word *roji* originally meant a passageway leading to a tea hut, and was represented by several Chinese characters with the same pronunciation. In the Edo period the characters signifying "dewy path" came to stand for *roji*, and a spiritual connotation was added to its meaning.

Tea gardens were also designed to provide a separate entrance to the tea house, for usually when entering the drawing room of a home, one had to come in through the front door and walk through a corridor or adjoining room, whereas with a garden one could enter straight into the tea house without disturbing the household. In addition, a special wooden gate was built in the garden.

According to a book by Ikenaga Sōsaku, a *sunoko* (veranda) was added to the house lest the guests leave their wet footprints on the tatami. For this reason tea gardens were an excellent innovation in that they helped to keep the houses clean and undisturbed.

As the years passed, tea gardens became larger. The first gardens were built by townspeople who had little land to spare for a tea garden, but when the tea ceremony was adopted by the samurai and nobles, there was more land available around their castles and palaces, and so the scale of tea gardens grew. New styles were then adopted, for example the double *roji*, in which a second garden was built outside the one surrounding the tea house, and the two were separated by a bamboo fence; or the triple *roji*, when a third garden was added around the other two.

A number of arbors were built in these gardens, such as *yoritsuki* (a place near the garden gate where the guests assembled and changed their clothes before the entertainment), and the *soto-machiai* (an arbor outside the *roji* where guests waited for their host). There were also other elements incorporated through the centuries, which I will mention briefly.

STEPPING STONES
Differing scales were used in the arrangement of stepping stones. Those laid out under Rikyū's direction were rather enormous, and were meant to afford easy walking. Rikyū's method was expressed in his saying: "A ratio of six for *watari* and four for *kei*." *Watari* means practicality, and *kei*, appearance, or artistic balance. Rikyū put more stress on practicality, while Oribe and Enshū held "four for *watari* and six for *kei*" as the ideal aesthetic proportions.

The difference between the two methods may be seen in two distinct garden arrangements. In the Myōki-an tea house designed by Rikyū, the stepping stones were arranged in a natural order, whereas those in front of the middle *shoin* of the Katsura Imperial Villa, said to have been laid out under the guidance of a tea master of the Oribe school, were arranged very differently.

Gradually the design of stepping stones came to follow established patterns. They were *niren-uchi*, *sanren-uchi*, *chidorigake gankō*, *nisan-uchi*, and *ōmagari*, according

166

to which stones of various sizes were placed taking into consideration their artistic balance with each other. At first mountain rocks were used, but later stones from the river and sea were included, and rare and curiously formed stones were particularly valued.

In *wabi* gardens, natural stones of medium size were sunk into the earth, but the stone path in daimyo-style tea gardens jutted out slightly. Large stones were placed at long intervals for the path through the outer *roji*, and small stones were placed at short intervals in the pathway of the inner *roji*.

PLANTS

The *roji* was planted with trees in order to suggest the atmosphere of a remote mountain. Trees such as pine, cedar and oak were selected, and shrubs and grass were planted around them. Flowering trees were avoided on purpose, for it was said that if one's eye were distracted by the *roji*, one's mind might be distracted from the mood of the tea ceremony. If one saw flowers growing in the garden, then those arranged so carefully in the tea room might not hold any charm in comparison. Over the years more rules were added. One of them was to avoid the use of plants which were fragrant, poisonous or thorny. Another rule was to use fewer trees and stones in a large *roji*, and more in a small *roji*.

Moss

Since early times the ground in most tea gardens has been covered with moss or bamboo bushes in order to remind the viewer of mountain scenery. Sometimes river sand or white sand might be spread on the ground in place of moss.

In the mid-Edo period a new method of producing ornamental designs, by arranging pine needles over sand, was employed. It called for a great amount of skill and hard work. Today pine needles are spread over moss in winter to protect it from the frost, but they are not used ornamentally.

The soil in the vicinity of Kyoto is especially good for the growth of moss. Since it is granitic in composition, it is well drained and always contains some moisture, which is necessary for raising moss. Among the many kinds of moss, the *sugi-goke* variety, which resembles a miniature tree and grows in foggy areas, is highly prized. This moss has a beauty distinct from most other varieties, and is cultivated very often in tea gardens.

THE MIDDLE GATE (*Chūmon*)

A gate was built to separate the inner and outer gardens. The host would walk through the gate to greet his guests, and it served to sever the outer world from the inner realm of tea.

At first the gate was a simple wooden structure but later, one with earthen walls and a small entrance came to be used. A hedge was grown beside the gate and also surrounded the garden.

THE WASH BASIN (*Tsukubai*)

One noteworthy element in the inner garden was a stone wash basin where guests rinsed their mouths and washed their hands before the tea ceremony, an act of purification before entering the tea room. Originally a standing wash basin was placed at the end of the veranda which adjoined the reception room so that it could be used without stepping into the garden. The basin was large and tall in keeping with the noble's custom of having his servant pour the water when he wished to wash his hands. After it was placed in the *roji*, however, it became shorter and smaller, and the guests crouched by its side in order to clean their hands by themselves. *Tsukubai* literally means "crouching."

Another reason for the use of a smaller basin and the shorter *tsukubai* is that the *sōan* tea ceremony required the host, before receiving his guests, to bring a pail of water with which to fill the wash basin. In other styles of wash basins a bamboo pipe would constantly refill the basin with water from a nearby lake or stream. Otherwise, it is the host's function to provide water.

Before long, there developed a prescribed arrangement for the stones near the *tsukubai*. On its right side is a flat stone, *yuoke-ishi*, where, in winter, a vessel of hot water is placed for the comfort of elderly guests. To the left, a tall stone called *teshoku-ishi* (lamp stone) is placed. This stone is used in the dawn tea ceremony or after dark. Sometimes the positions of the stones are reversed. While the inside of the basin is kept clean through constant care, the outside and the stones surrounding it are left covered by moss.

There is a rather interesting plumbing system devised for the wash basin, where one or two flat stones, called *mae-ishi*, are placed for the guests to kneel or crouch on while washing. Between these stones and the basin is the *suimon* (water gate), an indentation in the ground filled with pebbles or broken tile, which catches the overflow from the basin in the washing process. The pebbles (*gorota-ishi*) in this hole are kept clean by constant hand polishing, and the arrangement of these small pebbles is done with great care.

THE STONE LANTERN (*Ishi-dōrō*)

Stone lanterns were introduced to Japan from China and Korea through Buddhism, as they were first used in Buddhist temples, aud only later in Shinto shrines. According to written evidence, they were also used in ordinary gardens during the Muromachi period.

The stone lantern was used for lighting the inner tea garden, and was generally placed by the side of the wash basin, while smaller lanterns were placed in the garden. Sometimes only the lantern without the base was placed on the stone beside the wash basin. Great care was taken in the exact positioning of the stone lantern by the wash basin and the direction which it faced. According to the eleven volume *Kaiki* written in 1724, the light should fall onto the flat stones around the basin.

In the daytime the paper door of the lantern is lifted and the inside cleaned. At night an oil lamp is put into the lantern, shielded from the wind by the paper door. Various ideas were employed to provide more aesthetic effects; for example, on moonlit nights more wicks were added, while in snowy weather the light was not used at all. Thus stone lanterns are not merely garden ornaments or a means of illumination, but should also attract the admiration of the beholder when they are lit.

THE AREA AROUND THE GUESTS' ENTRANCE

A stone, called *fumi-ishi*, is placed in front of the guests' entrance and is raised slightly above the other stones. It is just high enough to enable the crouching guest's hand to reach the entrance, and its top is just wide enough to hold a pair of sandals. Since it is laid before such an important place, it is a carefully chosen stone, oblong, wider at the bottom, with features distinguishing it from other stones.

Another stone, placed a little lower than the *fumi-ishi*, is called *otoshi-ishi*, and in front of it another stone, *nori-ishi*, is placed. These three stones are arranged so precisely that the *nori-ishi* can be used to catch raindrops from the eaves of the tea house.

From this area in front of the guests' entrance, the garden path divides into two, one going in the direction of the *chiri-ana* (a pit to collect dead leaves), and the other toward the *katanakake-ishi* (a stone used for resting samurai swords). Stones of various shapes and sizes are arranged along both paths and pebbles are scattered around them.

THE PIT FOR DEBRIS (*Chiri-ana*)

The garden is always kept clean, but sometimes falling leaves from the trees or shrubs inevitably litter the garden after it has been swept. The leaves are picked up with special, green bamboo chopsticks and dropped into the *chiri-ana*. Originally it was supposed to be built in an unseen place, but later it came to be part of the area viewed by guests. Historical records say that a flower-decorated *chiri-ana* was seen

170

in the Momoyama period, but today's *chiri-ana* is distinguished only by a stone called *nozoki-ishi* (peeping stone), placed on one side.

The size of the *chiri-ana* varies in relation to the size of the tea house. The larger size is square, and the smaller type circular. The above-mentioned green bamboo chopsticks are laid beside it, and a few twigs from the garden are put into it for effect.

THE DISTINGUISHED GUEST'S ENTRANCE (*Kininguchi*)

Besides the *nijiriguchi*, the tea house has another entrance for the reception of distinguished guests, which also serves the purpose of letting light in. Such an entrance is closed over with paper sliding doors, and the stepping stone in front of it is higher and longer than the one used for other guests. Until the Momoyama era the tea house had either a *nijiriguchi* or a *kininguchi*, but never both, until much later.

THE STONE PATH (*Nobedan*)

This is another path through the garden, distinguished in its appearance by an alternation of oblong and small natural stones. The contrast between the artificially cut stones and the natural stones gives an interesting effect to the path like the famous Shin-no-tobi-ishi Path of the Katsura Imperial Villa.

THE WAITING ARBOR (*Machiai*)

In early times the veranda of the *shoin* was used as the waiting area, for instance the Sanun-jō room in Kohō-an, a temple within the compounds of Daitoku-ji in Kyoto. With the development of the *sōan* and its *roji*, the arbor became more of a separate house with benches provided inside. A stepping stone was placed before the bench in order to provide a place for resting the feet. The stone for a distinguished person or the principal guest was different from the others, either a little larger or placed higher and slightly apart from the others. In some places one long stone was used for all the other guests.

WATERING THE GARDEN

One of the rules of the tea ceremony, is that the garden should be kept fresh and green through constant sprinkling. This is done not only to enhance its beauty, but also to enable moss to grow. Great care is taken in the manner of watering, which is referred to in Japanese by the expression to strike water, rather than to sprinkle. Generally, the areas under the eaves, fences, walls and gates are watered. Even after rain, the lower portion of the gate and the wooden walls are watered. At the same time, this practice tells the guests that the host's preparations for the tea ceremony are complete. If one arrives at a *cha-no-yu* gathering to find that the garden has not been sprinkled, it is a sign that the host is not yet ready.

There are actually three fixed patterns of watering the garden during the course of a tea entertainment, known as *sanro*. The first sprinkling is carried out before the guests enter the tea room, the second, in the short recess between the first and second parts of the tea ceremony, and finally, it is done once more before the guests leave. Care is taken not to wet the *katanakake-ishi*, because swords must be kept from moisture, and the low-growing plants, which brush against the guests' clothes, are not watered either.

Thus far I have related some changes in the tea garden, its noteworthy features, and its care. Although I have not given detailed explanations, the tea garden, like the tea house, is divided into four types, and varies according to the taste and social status of the owner. At the same time, it must also be in harmony with the tea house: a plain garden suits a simple hut, and an elaborate landscape garden goes with a grand tea house. On page 208 there is a list of some representative tea houses and their gardens, so that the visitor to Japan may have some information on tea architecture and tea gardens in this country.

CONCLUSION

Cha-no-yu Today

Japan has recently made remarkable advances both in the economic and scientific sectors, but this progress has not been carried into the realm of the tea ceremony. On the contrary, the purity and simplicity of the art has diminished since commercialism has crept into this ancient skill.

In Rikyū's time, tea masters and their followers enjoyed the ceremony in a free, individualistic manner, although they were also keenly aware of the need to keep the art from degenerating or becoming mundane and vulgar. But the long reign of the Tokugawas soon confirmed their worst fears, as the new government began to recognize all the different schools of tea that existed at the time. They also improvised the *iemoto* system for the professions, which, as we have seen, changed the close personal relationship that had hitherto existed between tea master and students.

More changes followed later. A system of rank was imposed on the Buddhist religion, temples were graded according to government ruling, and each family had to belong to a certain temple. For this reason there was no individual choice in the matter of religion, and the chief temple had the power to prohibit the formation of any new sect by the people. This greatly strengthened the effect of the *iemoto* system in the religious field.

Although the influence of the *iemoto* system was not as great in the tea cult, it did, however, change the basic *raison d'être* of the tea ceremony. Only the *iemoto* of each school was entitled to grant a tea master the license to teach, and no pupil could aspire to become an independent teacher until he was given a tea name by the school. Those who were not independent could only learn the process of serving

173

tea from the *iemoto* and were later qualified to pass on only that skill to their students. And, as in the Momoyama period, tea masters were not allowed any scope for creativity, for if they innovated, they were ostracized from the school. Thus, one result of this system was the increase in the number of rules and steps of instruction, and tea schools came to be highly conservative in character and rigidly formal in practice. (An exception to this was the case of the *iemoto* which adapted its customs to those preferred by the influential daimyos or powerful merchants; but not many of them had a genuine feel for tea.)

As the tea ceremony was conducted privately and indoors, there was no opportunity for students of *cha-no-yu* to learn from each other, or to compare their performances as in the earlier days. And generally there was very little progress made (unlike the *iemoto* of the Nō drama, which being public, could entice a lot of criticism from the audience, and because of this the Nō actor perfected his art under the watchful eyes of his audience).

It also happened sometimes that the eldest son of a tea master was too young to succeed his father, or he did so just for the fame, but proved unable to fulfill his duty of handing down the art to his successors. But in these cases, there was a law which entitled the best student to succeed his master, and he would later on establish his own *iemoto*, but this did not prevent the sons, who were completely unqualified, form carrying on just the same.

The same unfortunate fate befell those who wanted to practice Zen meditation in order to discipline themselves, for this became another *iemoto* school specializing in one aspect of *cha-no-yu*. The teacher would pass on his skill to his sons, who were totally incapable of teaching meditation, but who persisted for the name. Men of learning, such as Matsudaira Fumai, were highly critical of these practices, and especially of the effect of *iemoto* in Kyoto, the ancient home of the tea ceremony.

While the *iemoto* system helped preserve the traditional art, it also caused the tea ceremony to be divided among many schools. It had previously consisted of one

174

body of thought, with intentions of creating bonds of harmony among its participants, and it resulted in clashes among the different schools. It had the disadvantage of confining the students' knowledge within the limits of a particular school, rather than freeing their minds to embrace the entire field of the tea ceremony.

It is most regrettable that this attitude persists today among those who are anxious, not to promote the art, but to bring leading statesmen and businessmen into their schools to promote their fame. And unless these commercial interests are abandoned, the future of *cha-no-yu* does not appear encouraging. Tea ceremony entertainments are held daily in Japan, and it is not unusual for two or three thousand people to assemble for a large gathering. Tea, today, is only popular among women, who regard its study as a necessary asset for marriage. As soon as they receive their diplomas, they discontinue their studies or get married, although a few may pursue the art of tea after their marriage as an expensive pastime.

Most of these women, who make up the majority of tea students today, learn only a part of *temae*, and not the theory or history of tea. This is natural since the tea ceremony cannot be performed without one having first mastered the proper procedure. Furthermore, there is more concentration today on the tea articles used, and it has become the aim of every student to use only impressive utensils, irrespective of their aesthetic value. It is the handling of the tea vessels which remains in the memory of the students, while the spiritual side of the ceremony is easily overlooked.

There are a few male students, mainly noted businessmen, who practice the tea ceremony because it has become fashionable to own a tea house, but not many of them pursue the art earnestly enough or are able to understand it as deeply as either Sugiki Fusai or Sen no Sōtan. They are quite content to leave all the preparations in the hands of their own tea master, although they can usually boast a fine collection of tea utensils. Other men interested in the art usually study its philosophy and history; very few will learn the performance.

The *iemoto* system is still strong today, and there is one school with over a million students, but interest in promoting the art of *cha-no-yu* for its own sake has few followers. The spirit of the art is gradually waning: department stores hold tea article exhibitions, where on-the-spot sale of utensils, mass-produced objects of art and glamorous kimono are considered appropriate for tea ceremonies. A small tea room is set up in one corner to attract buyers—a contrived tea room in a most improper setting!

The present trend of *cha-no-yu* has affected its participants, who seem to have forgotten the spirit of the tea ceremony amid the showy consumerism of today. It was during the turbulent period of the Muromachi era that *cha-no-yu* had its origins, when it served both as food for the mind and for the spirit, and by the same token it should still be flourishing today, since so much confusion distracts our everyday lives.

It is insufficient to dwell too much on etiquette and aesthetic appreciation, as the art of the tea ceremony can only be improved through the study of all its aspects, other than those which are superficial, materialistic, or easiest to master in a short period of time.

APPENDICES

NOTES TO PLATES

5.   Tai-an is the name of a very small tea house built in the *sōan* style underneath the shingle roof of Myōki-an, a Zen temple in Yamazaki, Kyoto. It is thought to have been constructed by Rikyū in 1582, and has been declared a National Treasure by the government of Japan. It is a rare example of the early structure of tea houses, with the small two-mat tea room and its alcove both covered with tatami. Adjacent to the tea room are two one-mat rooms partitioned off by papered sliding doors.

6–7.   The pathway underneath the eaves of the Tai-an tea house leads to a gate which opens onto another path that goes to the guests' entrance (*nijiriguchi*). The stepping stones buried in the path were arranged by Rikyū and have been left untouched. The size of the guests' entrance in the Tai-an is slightly larger than those built in later days.

8.   A view of the interior of the tea room with the guests' entrance shown on the left. In order to make the tea room look larger, the ceiling was constructed at different levels, which also determined the seating position of the host and guests. The ceiling just in front of the alcove, which is usually flat (*hira tenjō*), is reserved for guests, while the host's place (*temaeza*) has a lower sloping ceiling. But in the Tai-an, the height of the host's ceiling did not differ from that of the guests', but one side of the roof slopes downward, exposing the bare reed and bamboo ceiling.

The guests' entrance is shown on the lower left of the picture. Above it in the center is the latticework window, framed with bamboo. At the left, two layers of window can be seen, one of which is papered and slides open. The frame of the windows is usually made of wood in other tea houses, but in the Tai-an, it is of bamboo. The same type of windows is found in the other two one-mat rooms. These windows not only let in more light, but the visual patterns produced in the room when the rays of the sun penetrate the paper are especially pleasing.

The lower part of the wall is covered with paper so that the clothes of the guests do not come in contact with the rough mud walls. The height of the papered section depends on the builder, but it is usual for the guests' wall to be papered to a higher level than the host's. The paper used for the guests is generally dark blue (*minato-shi*), while that for the host is white (*mino-gami*). In earlier times it was also customary to cover the mud walls of the tea room with old writing paper in order to lend it more rusticity, but today such paper is very hard to come by. On the right, the one-mat room is just visible.

9.   When entering the Tai-an, the first feature that comes into view is the alcove. Rikyū, in his individualistic manner, plastered the inner walls of the alcove with mud and reduced the height of the alcove ceiling. The mud used to plaster the walls was mixed with straw to give the room more *wabi* atmosphere. Rikyū

179

used to hang the scroll directly against the rough wall instead of pasting protective paper behind it. The calligraphy on the scroll is by a high priest of the Azuchi-Momoyama period, Kokei Sōchin, who copied out test questions used in Zen training.

10. In the corner of the one-mat room are the hanging shelves used for storing tea utensils. Two smaller planks of wood are suspended by a bamboo pole from a larger shelf at the top of the wall.

11. The window beside the guests' entrance of the Tai-an is designed with the unplastered mud wall of a humble home in mind. Usually, in most tea houses, between one to seven reeds are bound together in a lattice pattern with wisteria vines, but in the case of the Tai-an, split bamboo pieces are added as well. The motif of bamboo is echoed by placing a pole vertically beside it, giving it both harmony and strength.

12. The Katsura Imperial Villa in Kyoto was first constructed by Prince Hachijō Toshihito and enlarged by his son Prince Toshitada in the mid-seventeenth century. The path leading from the front gate to the entrance of the main building is known as the Miyuki Path, and part of it, from the front gate to the middle gate, is covered with bluish black pebbles. The middle gate opens onto the inner garden and its path is built of cut stone covered with moss, beautifully arranged without any hint of artificiality. This path of irregular-shaped stones is referred to as Shin-no-tobi-ishi or "orthodox stepping stones," but the exact date of its incorporation into the garden of the Villa is unknown. However, the path reflects the taste of the nobility of that period, who generally preferred cut stone paths to Rikyū's simple, natural path.

13. These stepping stones sunk in soft moss meander along the path of the outer garden. Unlike the path in the inner garden, which is built along a straight line since it is supposed to guide guests to the tea house, this one is more suggestive of a leisurely walk to survey the scenery in the garden.

14. The New Goten is one of the buildings of the Katsura with its southwestern wings designed in a style similar to that of the elaborate and spacious palace in Kyoto called the Nijō-jō, which was specially built for the Tokugawa shogunate. The Katsura, with its thatched roof and one-storied design, does not give the same impression of grandeur, but, with the use of special pillars to level off the sloping land, it exudes a certain structural charm. Grass, covering the entire garden, gives an illusion of spaciousness, although in former days certain sports like *kemari*, a kind of football, horse racing and archery were practiced on the lawn.

15. The stepping stones of the Katsura Imperial Villa lead from the main building round the Middle Shoin and the Old Shoin, and into the Music Room located in the southwestern wing of the palace. The last portion of the stone path is shown in this picture, and the combination of turf, moss and stone arranged in a geometrical pattern is both beautiful and unique. The boundary between the moss and the turf is marked out by tiles, and pebbles are used to line the rain catchments, since the Shoin buildings do not have rain gutters underneath the roofs.

16. The Ichinoma or First Room of the New Goten consists of a six-mat room and a three-mat raised platform called the *jōdan-no-ma*. This room is also

180

known as the Miyuki Goten or Imperial Goten since it was specially constructed as a living room for the retired emperor Gomino-o and the empress Tōfukumon-in. The ceiling of the room is made of wood arranged in a latticework design, and in the left foreground, the fine, mulberry wood writing table is placed next to the wall shelves (*katsuradana*) made of beautifully grained wood, an eloquent expression of the aristocratic taste of the period.

17. The Shōkintei is the principal tea house in the Katsura Imperial Villa. It has a sloping thatched roof over the main building, which consists of an eleven-mat tea room, and on the left, just under the shingle roof, the guests' entrance to the tiny three-mat tea room can be seen. Before the ceremony, the guests walk along the stepping stones to the water's edge to wash their hands.

18. Boating was a popular recreation on the pond in the evenings, and stone lanterns were set on the water's edge to light the way for guests. The lanterns, built in a variety of styles in different periods of history, serve a functional purpose of lighting the way for boaters, and also add to the beauty of the garden at night.

19. Under the wide eaves of the Shōkintei, a special area designed for cooking is located, complete with fireplace (*kudo*) and draining board. It is uncertain to what extent the *kudo* was used, but the juxtaposition of the square and the circle in its design, and the combination of bamboo, reed and spice bush in the construction of the draining board, is especially pleasing.

20. Sections of the stone path leading from the gate of the Kohō-an, a temple built by Kobori Enshū for his family, is located in the Ryōkō-in, one of the minor temples of the Daitoku-ji in Kyoto. Apart from the temple, there is also a reception room, the living quarters called Jikinyūken, and the tea room called Sanun-jō. The garden, also constructed by Enshū, is famed for its "eight scenes," while the combination of cut stones and natural stones in the pathways of the gardens is aesthetically pleasing as well as easy to walk on.

21. Unlike the stepping stones in the Tai-an, these are buried into the path that leads along the wide porch to the reception room. This flat pathway is especially convenient for the elderly to walk on.

22. The theme in the design of the Kohō-an and its gardens is one that expresses movement. The eight scenes incorporated in the construction of the garden are suggestive of the changing views encountered on a boat trip. The grounds of the garden are supposed to represent either a river or a lake. To enter the reception room (Bōsenseki), one has either to go through the adjacent room or walk across the small patch of pebbles. The wide porch is designed with two steps, the lower one representing a mooring place for boats. The latticework sliding door above the steps of the porch is built to resemble the long windows found on boats, and the paper covering the window prevents direct sunlight from entering the room. Once in the room, the view of the garden changes once more. The stone lantern in the pebble patch is made of materials from three countries: the pedestal comes from India, the lantern from China, and the dome from Korea.

23. Just before the tea ceremony, it is the custom for the host and guests to wash their hands and rinse their

mouths with water from the stone wash basin. The one pictured here, a well-known one, has the word *roketsu*, meaning to make dew, carved on its side. The sunlight striking the water of the wash basin creates beautiful patterns of light and shadow on the ceiling of the reception room, while the pebbles on the ground glisten when washed by rain or lightly sprinkled with water.

24. The construction of the preparation area (*temaeza*) alongside the alcove was a style favored by Enshū. Its original design probably emphasized the decorative rather than the functional use of space, but as the view of the garden was more magnificent from this area, Enshū himself used to prepare and serve tea to his guests. There is an opening in the partition between the alcove and the preparation area through which a scroll of calligraphy by a priest called Kōun, can be seen from the *temaeza*.

25. The Ido tea bowl, with its rough texture and its large base, replaced the more elegant *temmoku* (brown-black Chinese style) tea bowls, for its appearance was more in keeping with the *sōan*-style tea ceremony. These bowls originally came from Korea, where they were used in everyday life, and only ten were brought to Japan in the late sixteenth century. Because of their age they were called Ōido or large Ido tea bowls. This one was named Kizaemon Ido, after one of its owners, Takeda Kizaemon of Osaka, in the early seventeenth century. It was also in the possession of Matsudaira Fumai for more than thirty years, although there is no evidence to say that he used it as a tea bowl. Finally, after changing hands several times, it was given a permanent place at the Daitoku-ji. Several interesting anecdotes are associated with its history. When the

bowl is viewed from the side, the shape is uneven, and the deep wheel marks on its surface are clearly visible. The black dots on its rim show the efforts made at repairing the bowl with lacquer.

26. It is usual for most tea bowls to have small lumps (*atome*) in the inside bottom, but in this case, they are noticeably absent. These lumps are specially made just before firing in the kiln to enhance the beauty of the bowls. In the case of the Kizaemon Ido, wheel marks also appear on the surface of the interior while the whole bowl, except for the base, is covered by a glaze, most of which has worn off round the rim and in the center due to frequent use in tea ceremonies.

27. The same wheel marks appear on the external surface of the tea bowl, converging at the base. The rim of the base is made uneven by a special spatula so that the glaze would not cover these rougher areas when the bowl was fired. Furthermore, as the heat of the kiln was not sufficient to melt the glaze completely, it solidified in parts and stuck to the bowl. This process (*samegawajō-no-kairagi*) is a characteristic of Ido tea bowls.

28. The first man to produce black Raku ware was a disciple of Rikyū's called Chōjirō, who produced numerous bowls in this rustic style suited to the atmosphere of the small tea hut. Raku ware was designed specially for the tea ceremony, and the wheel marks prominent in other bowls are absent in this type. This is due to the fact that the clay was kneaded flat, its edges turned up, and the bowl molded into shape with the fingers. It was then fired in the kiln after which either red or black glaze was applied. The black glaze used to coat this bowl was made from the powder of

black stones, and the process of covering the bowl with glaze was repeated two or three times.

Raku ware is still made by descendants of the original families, but today they are much too glossy and brilliant to resemble the somber tones of the Chōjirō creations. The black glaze which Chōjirō used contained yellow spots which cannot be reproduced today, due to the different construction of the kilns. The hallmark of the maker is always imprinted on Raku tea bowls, and the period in which they were made is therefore easily identified.

29. Honami Kōetsu was a great artist as well as a famed tea master of the Edo period who left behind a number of fine examples of his work. This red Raku tea bowl was probably used for memorial tea ceremonies, for its color, shape and outward appearance is specially designed to resemble the king of hell. It is named Jū-ō, after the king of hell in the Buddhist pantheon.

30. This bowl, used as a container for sweets or for the *kaiseki* meal, is called *dorabachi* or gong bowl, due to its resemblance to the gong. It was made in the Momoyama period, in the late sixteenth century, and comes from the kilns in the Mino region (present day Gifu Prefecture). It is known as Yellow Seto because of its dull golden luster and its granular glaze, which gives the surface an uneven effect known as "fried bean curd" (*aburage*), a typical distinguishing feature of this type of bowl. Patterns are scratched out on the interior with a wooden spatula, and the green and brown colors are produced with oxidized copper and iron pigments. The rim is cut out in a floral pattern, and the ornate effect of the design is balanced with a completely plain exterior.

31. Furuta Oribe, one of the famous disciples of Rikyū, made his tea utensils at the Seto kilns. His creations are distinguished by their startling distortion of shape and the use of lively colors, especially the copper-green glaze which he preferred. Oribe created tea caddies, tea bowls, incense burners, water jars, dishes, sake jars and this covered dish, which was specially made from red and white clay to give more effect to the overall coloring of the finished product. This dish was most probably used for the *kaiseki* meal or for *kashi* sweets, and both the interior and underneath of the lid are decorated with colorful patterns.

32. This eggplant-shaped tea caddy is named after its owner, the tea master Jūshiya Sōgo, who lived during the early sixteenth century. The tea caddy containing the powdered tea is always placed in a bag and displayed in the preparation room before the tea ceremony starts. When *temae* is performed, the caddy is taken out of its bag, which is always made of precious silk, brocade or damask. The caddy shown here was imported from China and has an ivory lid, with the surface underneath the lid plated in gold. Formerly it was customary to replate the gold each time the tea caddy was used. In this case, its owner had several lids and bags made, each one carefully wrapped in paper and stored in a special box for protection.

33. The tea scoop (*chashaku*) is used to transfer the powdered green tea from the caddy to the tea bowl when *temae* is performed. The first tea scoops were made of ivory and imported from China, but gradually more modest materials such as wood or bamboo came to be used instead. Bamboo was not only more suited to the *sōan* tea room but since it is not as hard as ivory it did not damage the other utensils. Tea masters also

came to make their own tea scoops, and their lack of training as craftsmen was compensated by their deep interest in design. This tea scoop made by Rikyū came to be the model of all future ones, with its rounded tip and a node placed at the center of the shaft. It is both bold and elegant, a fine example of Rikyū's taste.

34. Nonomura Ninsei was a potter of the mid-seventeenth century who was patronized by the nobility of the court. His use of color and the refined design of his creations were wholly representative of the taste of upper-class Kyoto. Most of his colors were reds, greens, blues and purples, although occasionally he added gold and silver to his designs to increase their brilliance. This incense case made by Ninsei is only four centimeters long, and it is, like all his products, more delicate in appearance than the Oribe wares, although he made use of wheel marks to give more depth to his products.

35. This flower container in the old Iga style was produced at the Iga kilns in modern Mie Prefecture. During the Momoyama period, pottery from Iga became popular and Oribe himself commissioned numerous vases and water jars from the Iga kilns. This vase, known as Ko Iga or Old Iga, is the most precious type of pottery from the region, with the aristocratic blue-green ash glaze typical of Iga ware. It is eccentric in shape yet lively in appearance, and the strong marks made by the spatula give it a powerful solidity most suited to the *sōan* tea ceremony.

36. Flowers are selected and arranged with a great deal of thought by tea masters, and the best displays are simple bouquets of no more than two or three flowers. When the vase is small, such as this one made in the Echizen kilns and hung on the rough wall of the alcove, delicate flowers, like the pink camellia and the winter hazel, are used. Furthermore, it is advisable not to use flowers that are in full bloom.

37. This *shoin*-style tea room was modeled on a fifteenth-century design and has an alcove decorated with both hanging scroll and flowers. To the right of the alcove are the shelves on which tea utensils are placed, and to the left is a writing desk beneath the window. This style of architecture is still used today in constructing the guests' room or the reception room of a tea house. The scroll hanging in the alcove is the work of the Chinese emperor Hui Tsung of the twelfth-century Sung dynasty; the green celadon vase with a single peony has handles of phoenix design. Placed on the shelves are five *temmoku* bowls, an incense burner on the upper shelf, and an ink case to the right.

38. The *daisu* or stand is where all the utensils needed for the performance of *temae* are placed. This one is lacquered and dates back to the Edo period. On top of the *daisu*, to the right, is the tea caddy in its bag placed on a tray, and to the left is a *temmoku* tea bowl with gold leaf pattern. The bowl rests on a stand known as the *temmoku dai*. On the lower shelf to the right is the green celadon water jar which has the pattern of a dragon imprinted on the interior. It is known as a "cloud and dragon" jar since the dragon stands out in bold relief when the jar is filled with water. In the center foreground is the metal waste-water jar, which is also used to hold the lid of the kettle, while behind it, is the container where the chopsticks and ladle are placed. To the left of the picture, the portable brazier and the kettle can be seen. A feather broom

184

used to clean the brazier before the start of the tea ceremony lies on the tatami. The feathers of rare birds are especially prized in these little brooms.

39.   It has been customary since ancient times to hang a scroll of calligraphy in the alcove during the tea ceremony. The earlier scrolls were those written by priests of the Sung (960–1278) and Yuan (1280–1368) dynasties who influenced the development of Zen Buddhism in Japan, and the style of their brush writing was readily copied by Japanese Zen priests. It was Rikyū who said that the scroll is the most important article of the tea ceremony, since it can be appreciated throughout the ceremony. The calligraphy shown is by a Chinese priest, Hu Kuan Shih Lien.

40.   This is an alcove of a *sōan*-style tea room where both the scroll and the flower vase are displayed. The calligraphy is a poem from the *Ogura Hyakunin Shū*, an anthology of one hundred poems of the seventh to thirteenth centuries, and was selected and written by Fujiwara no Teika of the Kamakura period. The flower in the bamboo container is a white camellia, chosen to match the mood of the room as well as the poem on the scroll. When the alcove is covered with tatami, it is usual to insert a thin board underneath the flower vase.

41.   These utensils are used for the *sōan* tea ceremony, where the lacquered cabinet is disposed of in favor of a simpler *wabi* style of serving tea. Because the room is smaller, there is more intimacy in the sharing of a cup of tea, especially in winter, when the fire pit (*ro*) is used to boil water. The wooden frame of the *ro* is made by the famous craftsman Kyūi. The precious utensils shown here are excellent examples of the *wabi* senti-

ment, for the personality of the host is reflected in the choice of tea articles. They are, from left to right: the ladle resting on the bamboo stand, the purple *fukusa*, the waste-water jar made specially for use in a *sōan* tea room from chipwood, the Ōido tea bowl named Mino, the silk bag of the tea caddy, the tea caddy called Rikyū Enza-katatsuki, the bamboo whisk, and the water jar. The latter has been declared an Important Cultural Property by the government of Japan, and comes from the famous Iga kilns. It is named Yabure-bukuro. The kettle in the fire pit is of orthodox (*shin-nari*) design.

42.   In the making of *koicha* a greater amount of powdered tea is needed to produce the thick syrupy consistency, and generally the thicker the tea, the more bitter it becomes. In this way the taste of the tea can be changed according to the volume of water added to the tea, and also depending on the way the tea is stirred and blended with the whisk. The temperature of the boiled water can be another factor influencing the taste of the tea, and in winter, when the *ro* is used, the temperature of the water is raised by keeping the lid on the kettle after the water has come to the boil, and only removing the lid when the water is ready to be scooped out.

43.   The portable brazier used during the summer months vary in shape and material used. Some are made of earthenware, some, iron or copper, and some, although very few, are made of gold or silver. The one pictured here is made of earthenware coated with lacquer and is the most common kind of *furo* used for tea ceremonies. It has a wide opening in front to show the burning charcoal and surrounding molded ash, over which some white ash has been carefully sprin-

kled. Great precision is required to mold the ash as well as to sprinkle the white ash, which, if done unevenly, will give the fire a dull, lifeless effect.

To start the fire, one piece of burning charcoal is first placed over the molded ash, and more pieces added when the guests are seated. By the time the host has finished performing *temae*, the kettle should be boiling, and the tea can be made immediately. When the ceremony is over, the host takes the ash spoon from the ash bowl and scrapes the surface of the ash in a curve, to show that the event is over and the ash will not be used again for other performances.

44. There are various ways of performing *temae*, but the most common one is *hira-demae* or basic *temae*, when the host prepares *koicha* while being silently observed by the guests. A light meal is served before the tea is drunk, during which time the host is busy boiling the water. When this is done, the water is added to the powdered tea, and a scented aroma pervades the entire room.

45. The smelling of incense has become one of the formalities of the tea ceremony today, and it takes place after charcoal has been added to the fire pit. The correct method to smell incense is to hold the incense burner in your left hand, with your right hand covering the top, and bring it close to your face. It is then passed on to the other guests. Inside the container there is a small piece of burning charcoal embedded in ash, over which the sticks of incense are placed. In some cases, a small piece of mica is placed between the ash and the incense sticks.

46. This is a stone used in a tea garden to direct the guest to the tea house. They are known as *sekimori* or "guard" stones, bound together with rope made of dried fern. When the stepping stones in the tea garden branch off in two directions, a *sekimori* stone placed on one path will indicate to the guest that he is not to take this route. Since it is customary to observe complete silence during the ceremony, the *sekimori* stones serve the purpose of directing the guests without the host having to speak at all.

47. In tea gardens there is usually a small arbor, built in the best position from which to view the scenery, where guests may rest before entering the tea house or during a recess in the ceremony. The arbor pictured here is in the large garden of the Katsura Imperial Villa and is built on a larger scale than most.

48. This is the entrance to the Hassō-no-kakoi tea room of the Shōkintei, a structure of several buildings in the Katsura Imperial Villa. The stepping stones lead to the pond where guests washed their hands before the ceremony. Underneath the shingle roof, to the left of the guests' entrance, there are two wooden shelves (*katana-kake*) on which the samurai placed their swords before entering the tea room.

49. This is a passageway between the tea room and the preparation room (*mizuya*) in the Shōkintei. The door leading into the tea room is dome-shaped and is a distinguishing feature of a small tea room. In some structures, there may be another entrance for the host or his assistants, in which case the dome structure would not be used. The frame is made of light wood, with Japanese paper pasted on both sides of the door. When the preparation room is lit, the paper becomes semi-transparent, giving the whole room a warm and pleasing glow.

50. This is the view of the tea room as seen from the guests' entrance. The pillar separates the tea room from the preparation area, both of which are usually combined in a small tea room. In contrast to Rikyū's Tai-an (shown in color plates 1–7), this room has many more windows to brighten it, reflecting the tastes of the samurai and nobility of the time. During the summer, when the fire pit is not used, it is covered with a tatami mat, but during the winter only a board is placed over it.

51. This is the place where food is prepared, which occupies one corner of the Gepparō tea pavilion near the Old Shoin in the Katsura Imperial Villa. As this room was not used very often, there was only one fireplace and some simple shelves built in it, but its simplicity does not detract from the harmony created with the surrounding buildings.

52. This preparation room was constructed at the end of the Edo period in the nineteenth century and was transported by the author into his own tea garden. The shelves are stocked with the necessary tea utensils neatly arranged in their proper places, and the whole room is cleaned frequently just in case an unexpected guest should arrive. Gas and water facilities were added to the preparation room by the author.

53. The author has placed a wash basin, made in the Momoyama period, in the tea garden which he designed and constructed himself. The host has to clean his hands and mouth before he goes out to greet his guests, while the guests do the same before they enter the tea house.

54. During a dawn tea ceremony, or one held in the evening, the stone lanterns in the garden are lit, and additional paper lanterns placed in the inner garden to guide the guests into the tea room. The host or hostess welcomes the guests with a candle in hand, and then returns to the tea room to wait for the guests who will first have to go through the cleansing ritual.

55. In instances when there is a short recess between the serving of *koicha* and *usucha*, the guests will wait in the arbor, and the host sounds a gong as a signal for them to reenter. At the sound of the first gong, the guests leave the arbor and wait for the succeeding strokes before entering the tea room. The number of strokes sounded depends on the number of guests present, while the tone of the gong can vary from soft to loud, depending on the way it is hit.

56. The food served for the *kaiseki* meal is very simple and consists of two kinds of soup and three types of side dishes. While the guests are eating, the host sits in the preparation room and waits for the proper moment to bring in the next tray of food. He does not have to look into the tea room but knows intuitively when the guests have finished one course.

57. The *kaiseki* meal is more a light snack than a filling meal, since the kinds of food prepared by the host are usually simple and the quantity rather small. The meal is brought on a tray and handed personally by the host to his guests. There is usually a bowl of rice, a bowl of soup and a dish of either vegetables or fish on one tray. As the host brings the tray to the guest, the latter advances forward on his knees to receive the tray, after which verbal greetings are exchanged. This procedure is repeated once more when the *kaiseki* meal is over.

58. Calligraphy is an important element of the tea ceremony, for not only do these scrolls of brush writing decorate the alcove, but they also convey spiritual satisfaction to the guests. Most tea masters practice calligraphy regularly, not necessarily to improve their writing technique but to understand the teachings of the earlier masters, whose works they copy.

59. Since the late sixteenth century, tea masters have made their own tea scoops to suit their individual tastes: the thinness or thickness of the stalk, the shape of the tips, all these can be designed in a style which best suits the touch of the host. Here, the author is adding the finishing touches to a tea scoop.

60. When the portable brazier is used in tea ceremonies, the host shapes the ash with a special spoon into the form of a crescent moon. This signifies that the ash is being used for the first time and will not be used again for other guests. Then white ash is carefully sprinkled over the molded ash, and great pains are taken not to let the white ash damage the design of the molded ash. If this should happen, the whole process will be repeated once more from the beginning.

61. In the making of *usucha* using the portable brazier (notes 61–68), the tea ladle is handled in a very special way. The host's gaze is fixed to the tip of the ladle, and moves downward, slowly and steadily, yet completely naturally, to concentrate on the middle section of the ladle, and then further downward in the same manner to concentrate on the lower section.

62. The tea scoop is wiped with the *fukusa* before and after *temae*, holding one end of the scoop. As it is a very delicate instrument, the wiping movement should be soft, but at the same time the tea scoop should be held very steadily so that in wiping it the tea scoop itself does not move. This can be accomplished by tensing the muscles of the abdomen and holding the tea scoop in front of the body, wiping it rhythmically.

63. The tea bowl is always wiped and cleaned before bringing it out to the guests. Before *temae*, the host pours hot water into it to warm the bowl, after which the water is poured out and the bowl wiped dry with a tea cloth. The host holds the bowl in his left hand and wipes it with his right, looking into the bowl as he would a mirror. The bowl must be held firmly, yet the movements of wiping it must be soft and even.

64. *Usucha* is placed in a lacquered tea caddy, and tea is made for one person at a time, unlike *koicha*, where enough tea for all the guests is made at once. Two scoops of powdered tea are placed in the tea bowl and hot water added. This is the usual quantity for one person. The host is careful that his movements in making tea do not seem heavy or lifeless.

65. The amount of boiling water used to make one portion of *usucha* varies with the season, the type of guests present, or the inclinations of the host. A novice is usually taught to measure the amount of water in relation to the ladle, but rigid rules alone cannot produce good, tasty tea.

66. After the hot water is scooped into the tea bowl, the handling of the ladle conforms to etiquette. Body and mind must be in complete harmony, just as when shooting an arrow from a bow, otherwise this movement will lose all its meaning.

67. After the water is poured into the kettle from the water jar, the ladle is handled differently. The host places it on the rim of the kettle keeping his right arm straight, echoing the straight line made by the handle of the ladle.

68. When boiling water is poured into the tea bowl for the making of *usucha*, the ladle is returned to the kettle (*kiribishaku*). Quick action is required here, and any hesitation would spoil the success of *temae*.

69. Before adding charcoal to the "firing pit" (notes 69–72), all the other utensils should be in their proper places and the kettle removed from the brazier. The kettles come in a variety of shapes and sizes, although a big and solid-looking kettle is generally preferred. As the kettle is full of water at this stage, it requires steadiness and balance to lift it off the brazier. Once more the stomach muscles should be tensed in order to ensure that the kettle does not wobble while it is being moved.

70. The ash in the fire pit is arranged differently from that in the portable brazier. In the fire pit, damp ash rather than white ash is scattered over the surface of the molded ash. This process must be done with great precision so as not to disturb the shape of the molded ash in the pit.

71. To start the fire in the pit, the largest piece of charcoal, called *dōzumi*, is placed first in the pit. As the charcoal is too large to be handled with the pair of metal chopsticks (*hibashi*), it should be picked up with one's fingers. This is one reason for washing the charcoal pieces beforehand. The smaller pieces are then picked up and placed in the pit using the metal chopsticks.

72. The charcoal is cut into different shapes and sizes ranging from long to round to cleft or cut pieces. In accordance with the rules of the tea ceremony, different shapes are placed in the fire pit at specific times during the heating of the pit. Here the host places a piece of round charcoal called *kudazumi* into the fire pit with metal chopsticks.

73. A lot of the preparation for the tea ceremony is made before the guests arrive—for example, the cutting up of charcoal, the collection of ash to be used for the fire pit or portable brazier, and the sweeping of the tea room. Charcoal is cut into a variety of sizes, and depending on whether the fire pit or portable brazier is used, into a variety of different shapes.

74. The preparations for making *koicha* (notes 74–79) are more complicated than those for making *usucha*, since the *fukusa* used to wipe the tea caddy is handled differently. The tea caddy is usually a precious piece of ceramic ware, and for protection it is put inside a special bag made of silk or brocade. Each tea caddy can have several bags to suit the different occasions for its use, but the shape of the bag is generally determined by the size of the tea caddy.

75. The *fukusa* is handled very carefully since one of the reasons for cleaning the tea scoop, the tea caddy and the tea bowl is to instill into the guests a feeling of peace and tranquillity, conveyed through the host's movements in handling the *fukusa*.

76. The powdered green tea used for making *koicha* is placed in the tea caddy, and the quantity is determined by the number of guests present. To transfer the green tea from the caddy into the bowl, the host

first puts three scoops of tea into the bowl and then pours the rest directly from the caddy into the bowl. It takes experience to judge the exact amount of powdered tea needed for the number of people, since the taste of tea changes if the quantity of powdered tea is too much or too little.

77. Before making tea, the tea bowl and the tea whisk are warmed by pouring boiling water into the bowl and immersing the tips of the whisk in it. The correct measure of water used for this purpose is half a ladle, and the procedure remains the same whether the fire pit or the portable brazier is used. In winter, the tea bowl is first warmed in the preparation area before it is brought out to be heated once more with boiling water.

78. *Koicha* is made differently from *usucha*, since the mixture of powdered tea and water is blended with the whisk until it turns thick and syruplike. In the case of *usucha*, the mixture is beaten rapidly with the whisk until it begins to bubble and foam on the surface.

79. When the tea is ready for drinking the host offers the bowl first to his chief guest by placing it on the tatami mat in front of him. In the case of *koicha*, a small piece of silk or brocade is placed underneath the bowl.

80. After the tea has been drunk, it is customary for the guests to ask to be shown a few utensils by the host. These articles usually include the tea bowl, the tea caddy and its bag, and the tea scoop, which are placed in a convenient position on the tatami so that the guests may inspect them closely.

81. Before the tea is prepared, the guests are served with sweets made from red bean paste called *an*. As they are rather large, they are picked up with a pair of chopsticks and placed on a small piece of tissue paper before eating.

82–83. Since only one tea bowl is used in the tea ceremony, the rim of the bowl is wiped with the thin tissue and then passed on to the next guest. If the next guest is a member of the opposite sex, the bowl is placed on the tatami between the two persons and picked up by the next one, but in this case, the bowl is transferred by hand to the next guest.

84. This is a tea ceremony held out of doors which originated in the time of Hideyoshi, who used to bring his tea articles with him to the battlefield to enjoy a tea ceremony during a lull in the fighting. He was also accustomed to inviting large gatherings to his tea ceremonies which were held out of doors, either in palatial gardens or in the mountains. This type of ceremony can be performed at any season of the year, and here the author is making tea during the cherry-blossom season in the Kitayama area in the outskirts of Kyoto. He carries a portable brush and ink set with him.

190

A GUIDE TO TEA HOUSES

KYOTO

Daitoku-ji is a collective name designating the main temple and numerous small temples found within its compound, some of which possess tea houses which are mentioned below. The temples are listed first in alphabetical order and the names of the tea houses follow.

DAITOKU-JI: GYOKURIN-IN
KASUMIDO-NO-SEKI

This is found in the same building as the Sa-an (see below) but is designed in the larger *shoin* style. Its four-and-a-half-mat size makes it also the smallest of the *shoin* tea rooms. The alcove is about two meters high, incorporating shelves and, below them, a scroll painting of Mt. Fuji. These shelves have been specially placed in order to give an impression that the summit of Mt. Fuji is shrouded in mist, for the name of the tea house literally means "room of mist." The architectural style is, more accurately, a combination of *shoin* and *sōan* characteristics.

DAITOKU-JI: GYOKURIN-IN
SA-AN

The Sa-an tea house was constructed in 1741–43 by Kōnoike Ryōei. The design of the house was in keeping with the taste of the wealthy merchant class of the time, but it is interesting to note that an attempt has been made to preserve a *wabi* feeling by mixing cut rice stalks with mud to plaster the walls of the tea room. The pillar in the room is made of red pine log whose bark has not been removed, and a thin wooden plank is placed between the tatami where *temae* is performed and the tatami where the guests are seated.

DAITOKU-JI: JUKŌ-IN
KANIN-NO-SEKI

A simple tea room built in the style that Rikyū cherished is located in the Jukō-in, a temple constructed in 1573 by Miyoshi Yoshitsugu and founded by the priest Shōrei. It is said that Rikyū used to sit and meditate in this temple, and his grave and those of his family lie within the temple grounds.

DAITOKU-JI: KOHŌ-AN
BŌSENSEKI

Originally built by Kobori Enshū, the Bōsenseki was destroyed by fire in the mid-Edo period and reconstructed by Matsudaira Fumai (see color plates 20–24). It is an excellent example of Enshū's originality and creativity for the whole building is built to resemble a boat. The latticework sliding door above the porch looks like a boat's window, and is used not only to cut off the outside view but to prevent sunlight from entering the room from the west. Alongside the alcove there is a preparation area built according to the aristocratic taste of the time. The name comes from a poem by Chuang Tse, the famous Chinese writer and philosopher.

DAITOKU-JI: KOHŌ-AN
SANUN-JŌ
This, like the Bōsenseki, was also reconstructed at a later date, and is a good illustration of the tea room preferred by the nobility for their samurai guests. It is constructed in a mixture of *shoin* and *sōan* styles, and there are two entrances to the room, one through the inner garden, the other through the adjacent *shoin* room.

DAITOKU-JI: KŌTŌ-IN
SHŌKŌ-KEN
This tea room, simple in style and austere in decoration, was built by a disciple of Rikyū who followed his master's teachings on *wabi*. Hosokawa Sansai also constructed the Kōtō-in, which was completed after his death. The present building today has been largely remodeled and bears little resemblance to the original.

DAITOKU-JI: RYUKŌ-IN
MITTAN-NO-SEKI
Part of the *shoin*-style tea house of the Ryūkō-in was designed by Enshū and later remodeled. An alcove called Mittan-doko was specially designed to house the ink scrolls of the Chinese priest Mi An Hsien Chieh which Enshū possessed. Only one of his scrolls is in existence today, but it was highly valued even in Enshū's time, hence the special alcove. There is another alcove in the same room, where a scroll bearing Rikyū's seal of authentication is hung.

DAITOKU-JI: SHINJU-AN
TEIGYOKU-KEN
The tea room is built next to the reception room and is believed to be the work of Kanamori Sōwa. On going in through the guests' entrance, there is an earthen floor where the sword rest and the wash basin are located, a peculiar feature of this house, since usually these two objects are found outside the tea room. The interior divides into two sections by means of the papered sliding door which makes the room look larger.

GINKAKU-JI: TŌGU-DŌ
DŌJIN-SAI
The Ginkaku-ji or Silver Pavilion was built by Ashikaga Yoshimasa, who had originally planned to decorate it with silver, but whose death put an untimely end to this project. Of the original edifices only the Ginkaku-ji and the Tōgu-dō, constructed in the fifteenth century and containing a special room for the Buddha image, have survived. The tea room in the Tōgu-dō is called the Dōjin-sai, which is fitted with shelves, a side window and a fire pit. It is four and a half mats in size and is thought to be the original tea room constructed at that time. The garden of the Silver Pavilion with its famous well called Ochanomizu was designed by Sōami.

IMPERIAL PALACE (SENTŌ GOSHO)
YUSHIN-TEI
The building in the garden of the palace originally belonged to the Konoe family, but was moved to its present location in 1884. The roof is made of thatch, and the large crescent window in the tea room makes it unusually well lit.

KATSURA IMPERIAL VILLA
GEPPARŌ
This tea house (see plate 51) was used more often for moon-viewing than for tea-drinking, and so the decor was kept very simple. The preparation room consists only of a fireplace and some simple shelves.

KATSURA IMPERIAL VILLA
SHŌKINTEI

There are several tea houses in the Katsura Imperial Villa but the thatch-roofed Shōkintei is the only formally constructed tea house (see color plates 17–19, 48–50). The main building is surrounded by deep eaves on three sides, and along the facade of the building is a porch where a cooking area, preparation area and shelves are located. Usually the kitchen facilities are hidden from view, but in the Shōkintei they are boldly presented for all to see.

KŌMYŌ-JI: SAIŌ-IN
YODOMI-NO-SEKI

This tea house was built by Fujimura Yōken in the latter half of the seventeenth century and named after the Yodo River which can be seen from the window. The preparation area is separated from the guests by a dividing wall and a papered sliding door, named *dōan kakoi* after its inventor, Dōan, son of Rikyū. This is the only example of Dōan's creation in existence today. The sliding door is opened when all the utensils necessary for *temae* have been carried into the tea room, and closed when *temae* is over.

MANJU-IN
HASSŌ-KEN

This temple was originally constructed at the end of the eighth century and was transferred to its present location in the mid-seventeenth century, since which time a small *shoin*, a large *shoin*, a tea house and garden have been added. The style of the tea room is very similar to the Hassō-no-kakoi of the Katsura Imperial Villa, since its owner, Prince Ryōshō, was related to the Hachijō princes, builders of the Katsura Imperial Villa in Kyoto.

MYŌKI-AN
TAI-AN

This tea house (see color plates 5–11) is frequently attributed to Rikyū but this fact has never been verified. Yet, the bold composition of the tea room and its *wabi* atmosphere strongly suggest the hand of the great master. The walls surrounding the alcove are covered with mud, a style created by Rikyū. Of all *sōan*-style tea houses in existence, the Tai-an is the oldest, and has been designated a National Treasure.

NANZEN-JI: KONCHI-IN
HASSŌ-NO-SEKI

The tea room was designed by Enshū in 1628 at the request of the abbot of Konchi-in. The tea room is separated from the drawing room by a pair of papered sliding doors, and although the word *hassō* implies that there are eight windows, the tea room has only six of them. Unlike most tea houses, the passage leading to the guests' entrance does not go through the inner garden, but along the porch.

NINNA-JI
HITŌ-TEI

This tea room was built at the end of the eighteenth century on the command of Emperor Kōkaku. Although the design of the room conforms to *sōan* patterns and has a thatched roof, the tea room has two separate entrances, one of which was used exclusively for the nobility. The ceiling is rather high and has a round window, another reflection of contemporary aristocratic taste.

NINNA-JI
KYŌKAKU-TEI

This building was originally in the garden of a private

residence and was transferred to the temple during the first half of the nineteenth century. The tea room is identical in design to the Jo-an tea room in the Kennin-ji in Inuyama City, Aichi Prefecture. Next to the tea room there is another room which is not screened off by sliding doors, and both can be used in conbination to form a large tea room.

NISHI HONGAN-JI
IKUJAKU-NO-SEKI
This tea room is attached to the Hiunkaku, which was built by Hideyoshi in the Jurakudai and was removed to its present site later on. The tea room, completed in 1706, has large windows beside the alcove overlooking the pond in the garden. It has a special area covered with wood inside the room close to the guests' entrance which was used by the lords' retainers. The shelves used for *temae* are also built next to the guests' entrance.

NISHI HONGAN-JI
SHIRO SHOIN (OR SHIRO JOIN)
Constructed toward the end of the sixteenth century, the tea room is called by the same name as the one in Nijō Castle. The tea room faces a large reception room, and although colored paintings adorn the walls of the alcove, the room itself is by no means elaborate.

ROKUON-JI (KINKAKU-JI)
SEKKA-TEI
The temple formerly belonged to the Saionji family, but was purchased by Ashikaga Yoshimitsu in the fourteenth century who made it into a mountain retreat. The tea house was designed by Kanamori Sōwa in a country style with thatched roof, earthen floor and a fireplace built into it. At the end of the

nineteenth century the Sekka-tei was destroyed by fire but it was reconstructed soon afterward according to the original design.

SAIHŌ-JI
SHŌNAN-TEI
This is a building in the garden of the temple, with a tea room located in one corner. The building itself is said to have been restored in the seventeenth century by Sen no Shōan, who planned to retire there in his old age. Although it is built in the *sōan* style, there are papered windows and doors which can be opened to view the scenery in the garden, unlike other *sōan* tea huts. The garden, popularly known as Kokedera, or Moss Temple, because of the thick layer of moss which carpets the entire garden, is planted with beautiful trees and carefully laid out with a pond to enhance the view.

YABUNOUCHI HOUSE
ENNAN
This tea room is located within the residential quarters of the principal of the Yabunouchi School of Tea in Kyoto. It was originally built by Furuta Oribe, but was destroyed by fire in 1865 and rebuilt two years later. It is designed in the *sōan* style with a thatched roof, and one of its unusual characteristics is the triple *roji*.

TOKYO
SENSŌ-JI: DENPŌ-IN
TENYŪ-AN
The tea house was built by a tea devotee from Nagoya and was transferred twice before it found its final resting place in the Sensō-ji, in Asakusa, Tokyo. It was styled after the Fushin-an, a tea house owned by the

Omotesenke School of Kyoto, and is the oldest replica of the Fushin-an in existence today.

OSAKA
MINASE SHRINE
TŌSHIN-TEI

The Minase Shrine is located near the palace of the former emperor Gotoba, who, after abdicating his throne, often went to the palace to view the moon and the beautiful scenery around the palace. In the Edo period, the former emperor Gomino-o built a tea house in that area. It is constructed in the *sōan* style, but its interior is more lavish with an alcove, shelves and large windows. The ceiling is exposed and woven in a lattice pattern from seven different types of grass.

KANAZAWA, ISHIKAWA PREFECTURE
YŪGAO-TEI

The present tea house was remodeled from an earlier construction, and the large plot of land on which it was situated has now been converted into Kenroku Park. The tea house is built beside the pond and contains a very bright and spacious tea room.

MATSUE, SHIMANE PREFECTURE
KANDEN SAN-SŌ
KANDEN-AN

This tea room was built in 1792 by Matsudaira Fumai, in the villa of his chief retainer, in order to enjoy tea when he returned from a hunting trip. Fumai would enter the tea room after he had had a bath and changed from his hunting clothes. Unlike the Enshū style, Fumai's tea room is famed for its simplicity, and the Kanden-an is one of the very few tea rooms in existence today which was designed by Fumai.

KANDEN SAN-SŌ
KŌGETSU-TEI

The Kōgetsu-tei is located next to the Kanden-an and was built around the same time. The fire pit is built in the *daime* tatami, and the shelves next to the alcove are of a highly original and creative design. The style reflects a combination of *wabi* and fashionable samurai taste. The garden is covered with pebbles and laid out with stepping stones, and the view of the moon from the shrubbery is especially beautiful.

INUYAMA, AICHI PREFECTURE
JO-AN

This tea house was built by Oda Uraku in 1618 inside the grounds of the Kennin-ji in Kyoto. It was transferred to Tokyo in 1908, and then to Ōiso, Kanagawa Prefecture, and finally brought to Inuyama in 1971. It has one unusual aspect, which is the bamboo pole across its window, and the lower portion of the walls are covered with old paper calendars.

GLOSSARY

akatsuki no chaji: the name of the dawn tea ceremony held during the coldest season of the year. Guests arrive between three and four in the morning to observe *sumi-demae*, or the lighting of the fire pit with charcoal. The host usually greets his guests in the garden with a candlestick in hand, and there is an exchange of candles between host and guests.

asa-cha: the early morning tea ceremony held during the summer months before the sun gets too hot for comfort.

bokuseki: scrolls of calligraphy written by Zen priests, which usually convey philosophic religious themes. Some of the oldest examples, most cherished by tea masters, date back to the Sung dynasty of China in the eleventh century.

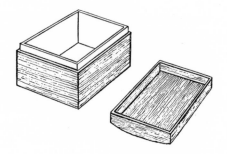

chabako: literally tea box, which contains all the tea utensils, except the waste-water jar, necessary for the ceremony.

chabana: the special floral arrangement for the alcove of the tea room which differs from *ikebana* in its use of only one or two flowers placed by the host in a simple container during the progress of the tea ceremony.

cha-e: an early name for the tea ceremony, which originated from the practice of tea-drinking in Buddhist temples and gradually spread to the general populace toward the end of the fourteenth century. As the etiquette of tea-drinking developed, various names were given to the ceremony, one of which is the more popular name *cha-no-yu*.

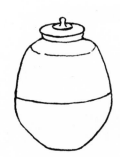

cha-ire: the container for powdered tea, used only in the making of *koicha*. There are various styles and shapes, but their distinguishing feature is the ceramic from which they are made.

196

chakin: the white piece of linen used for cleaning the tea bowl, before and after tea is served. It is soaked beforehand, wrung and folded in a prescribed manner.

chasen: the bamboo tea whisk used for kneading or stirring the powdered tea after water has been added. It is warmed in water first to prevent the fine bamboo spokes from splintering during use.

chashaku: the ladle used for scooping powdered tea from the caddy into the bowl. Originally these ladles were made of either ivory or metal, but now are most often of bamboo. Most tea masters carve their own, and some of the older ones still bear the name of the carver, the name given to the article, and some facts relating to its history. It is customary to use the most appropriately named tea ladle for a special tea ceremony.

chashitsu: literally tea room, whose shape, size, design and decoration varies according to current fashion. Today there are two kinds, the large room and the small room, which are most frequently used.

chigaidana: asymmetrical shelves built beside the alcove where stationery, incense sticks or even books are displayed.

chiri-ana: a pit dug into the ground close to the tea house in which fallen leaves from the inner garden are picked up with long bamboo chopsticks and placed. Its purpose is both practical and ornamental, and to enhance its attractiveness, a stone is placed alongside it together with the pair of long chopsticks across.

chūmon: the middle gate built between the inner and outer garden where the host greets his guests before the start of the tea ceremony.

daisu: stand or cabinet used for grand, formal tea ceremonies. Originally introduced from China, it is either made from plain or lacquered wood, and differently named according to its shape or design.

daime tatami: a rush mat, shorter than the usual tatami mat.

dora: a metal gong that is struck as a signal for the guests to either enter the tea room, or in the case where a short recess occured, to reenter the room.

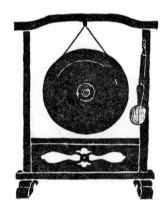

fukusa: a square piece of expensive silk used to clean the tea caddy and the tea scoop before tea is made. The host can also use it to hold the hot lid of the kettle.

fumi-ishi: stepping stones leading toward the guests' entrance where the sandals are kept when removed. Usually great care is taken to choose a large stone with a flat top. The small stones placed in front of the bench in the waiting arbor are also called by this name.

furo: the portable brazier used during the warmer months to heat the kettle, which can either be made from iron, bronze, silver or ceramic, and named according to its shape and size.

futa-oki: a small piece of metal or ceramic on which the ladle or the kettle lid is placed. For the least formal tea ceremony, a bamboo *futa-oki* is most often used.

gorota-ishi: a mass of variously shaped pebbles piled up between the stone wash basin and the front stone.

hachi: a shallow or deep container in which food and sweets are placed, made either of wood or porcelain.

hana-ire: a flower vase most commonly made of ceramic, metal or bamboo, which is either placed on the alcove floor, hung on the pillar beside the alcove or suspended from the alcove ceiling, depending on the size of the tea room.

katsugama: the first tea ceremony of the year usually held either on the fifth or sixth day after New Year's Day.

hibachi: a fireplace in the waiting room over which a kettle is placed.

198

hibashi: a pair of long metal chopsticks used for putting large pieces of charcoal into the fire during the preparations for boiling water.

higashi: small dry cakes with a sandy texture served with *usucha*.

hiroma: a name applied to a room larger than four-and-a-half mats suited for larger gatherings of guests. The design of the room differs from the smaller tea room and the alcove is fitted with numerous shelves to hold all the utensils necessary for the ceremony.

ishi-dōrō: a stone lantern which originated in China and was originally used in the gardens of temples and shrines. In the early Muromachi period it was placed in ordinary gardens not only for decoration but also to illuminate the garden during evening tea ceremonies.

kaiseki: the light meal served at the start of the tea ceremony before *koicha* is drunk, so named because monks in Buddhist training placed small heated stones on their stomachs to relieve hunger when fasting. The meal itself usually consists of two kinds of soup and three plates of fish and vagetables as well as sake.

kaishi: a small piece of thin tissue paper used either for holding sweets or wiping the rim of the tea bowl before passing it on to the next guest. The *kaishi* used by men is slightly larger than that for women.

kama: the kettle used for boiling water, usually made of iron, although silver and gold kettles are also produced. They are often called by the name of the area in which they are made or after the owner or craftsman.

kakemono: hanging scrolls of works of art or calligraphy that decorate the tea room alcove.

kōboku: pieces of aromatic wood, aloeswood and sandalwood, which are added to the charcoal fire when the portable brazier is used during the tea ceremony. The wood was first imported from China and incense-smelling was later adopted as one of the formal procedures of the ceremony.

199

kobukusa: sometimes called a small *fukusa* on which the tea bowl is rested when drinking tea. It is used only when *koicha* is drunk and is usually made from precious silks or brocades.

koicha: the thick tea made from the buds of tea shrubs which are between thirty to eighty years old, although the leaves of younger trees that have been protected from the sun can also be ground into powder. A greater quantity of powdered tea is used in the making of *koicha* than *usucha* since the texture has to be thick and pasty.

mae-ishi: or front stone is placed just in front of the stone wash basin where the guests crouch to rinse their mouths and wash their hands with water from the basin.

mei: a name given to almost all the articles in the tea room such as tea bowls, caddies, scoops, incense burners. It is customary to use those utensils whose names suit the occasion or season during which the ceremony is held. It is also usual for the guests to inquire from the host the details of the name, origin or date of the tea articles under inspection at the end of the ceremony.

mizusashi: the water jar used for the tea ceremony, made of either metal, ceramic or wood.

nakadachi: the short recess between the *kaiseki* meal and the *koicha* service, during which time the guests relax for a while in the waiting arbor or waiting room in the inner garden and wash their hands, while the host tidies up the tea room in preparation for the second part of the tea ceremony.

namagashi: soft cakes filled with sweet bean paste, larger in size than *higashi* and eaten with *koicha*.

natsume: the lacquered tea caddy which is used for the serving of *usucha*. Originally, only certain shapes of these caddies were so named, but gradually all lacquered tea caddies were referred to by this name.

nerikō: a mixture of various types of incense which is burnt and smelt by the guests after the charcoal fire is lit in the course of the tea ceremony. There are special incense cases and incense burners used for this purpose, although when the fire pit is used, incense is added to the charcoal.

nijiriguchi: the small raised guests' entrance to the tea room through which the guests have to crawl.

nobedan: a paved walk in the garden surrounding the tea house which is made of natural or hewn stone carefully arranged in a geometrical pattern.

Raku ware: the most renowned of all tea ceremony ceramics is produced in a district near Kyoto. The present master is the fourteenth descendant of its founder, and famous artists such as Kōetsu have left a number of masterpieces of Raku pottery.

renji mado: a window with two papered sliding doors, and a bamboo latticework frame outside it.

ro: a fire pit, built and sunk into the floor of the tea room, used during the cold season instead of the portable brazier.

roji: the inner garden of the tea house where the waiting arbor, stone wash basin and paved footpath are constructed and laid out with great precision. More elaborate tea gardens have both an inner and an outer *roji*.

sarei: the formal etiquette for tea-drinking observed in Zen temples that was introduced from China in the eleventh century, along with the method of manufacturing powdered tea.

sekimori-ishi: a small stone or stones bound with hemp rope laid on the stepping stones in the *roji*, usually where there is a forked path, to guide the guests towards the tea house.

sensu: a folding fan which is used to greet the host or other guests on arrival at a tea ceremony. In the tea room, a fan placed before a person's knees signifies his respect for the others present.

shifuku: a bag to protect precious tea caddies or tea bowls, usually made from satin damask or silk crepe, themselves objects of appreciation.

shoin: originally this was a study or writing room in the Zen temple occupying a small projecting sector of the room, but later it was adopted into the design of private homes where the *shoin* room replaced the drawing room, and ornamental shelves and alcoves were built in it. Later on a desk was also incorporated into the design of the drawing room, usually located just beneath the window.

shozumi: the placing of charcoal into the portable brazier or fire pit, a part of the tea ceremony which is performed in front of the seated guests.

sōan: a tea hut built from natural materials to resemble a farmhouse is used for the simplest, least affected style of tea ceremonies.

soto-machiai: or outer waiting room, provided for the guests to wait for the host to meet them before the ceremony begins. It is considered more proper to provide a waiting room in the outer garden as well as a waiting arbor in the inner garden, but in less formal ceremonial styles, the waiting room serves both functions.

suibokuga: paintings done with india ink and characterized by a harmonious blend of light and dark shades of ink. They were popular during the T'ang and Sung dynasties of China and were introduced to Japan during the Kamakura period by Zen monks. Painters of *suibokuga* during the Muromachi were almost all priests.

sumi-demae: after the first piece of burning charcoal is placed in the portable brazier or fire pit, the host adds charcoal three more times to keep the kettle boiling.

temae: a ceremonial way of preparing and serving tea according to rule.

temmoku: tea bowls covered with a special brownish black glaze, with narrow bases and broad rims produced in Fukien Province in China and highly prized by tea masters. Since the Edo period, these bowls have come to be used on very formal occasions when tea is offered to Shinto or Buddhist deities or members of the nobility. It is thought that the name derives from Mount Temmoku, where the first priests who went to China to study found them and brought them to Japan.

temmoku-dai: a rather tall saucer on which a *temmoku* tea bowl is placed, which was also introduced to Japan from China. The saucers are made from plain wood, lacquer or leather.

tenugui: a cotton towel, long and narrow in shape, used to dry the hands and mouth after rinsing them with water from the stone wash basin before entering the tea room.

tokonoma: the alcove in either a tea room or drawing room that is decorated with objects of art, most usually a scroll of calligraphy or a painting, a vase of flowers or an incense burner. The construction of these alcoves varies with the overall design of the room or house.

yobanashi: a special tea ceremony held from the early evening late into the night during the cold season when the fire pit is used instead of the portable brazier.

yoritsuki: a room in the main house where guests meet to change their clothes and wait for the other guests to arrive. It is sometimes built separately in the outer garden.

yūzari: a tea ceremony held from the early evening late into the night during the warm months when the portable brazier is used.

zenseki: name given to the first half of the tea ceremony which occurs just before the short recess.

CHRONOLOGICAL CHART

YEAR	EVENT	TEA DEVOTEES
A.D. 607	Japanese mission sent to the Sui emperor of China	
618	Beginning of the T'ang dynasty of China (618–905)	
630	First mission from Japan sent to China under the T'ang dynasty	
710	Beginning of the Nara period (710–84), capital transferred to Nara	
729	Emperor Shōmu holds *incha*, a religious ceremony when tea is served to Buddha or the emperor	
760	The first work on tea, *Cha Ching*, is written by Lu Wu	
784	End of the Nara period	
794	Beginning of the Heian period (794–1192), capital transferred to Kyoto	
805	Tea seeds brought from China by Saichō, a priest, and planted at Hiyoshi Shrine in Sakamoto, Ōmi, near Kyoto, the oldest tea plantation in Japan	
815	Emperor Saga visits Karasaki, Ōmi, and is served boiled tea by the priest Eichū	
905	Fall of the T'ang dynasty of China	
942	The priest Kūya treats sick people with tea	
960	Beginning of the Sung dynasty of China (960–1278)	
1053	*Cha Lu* is written by the Chinese calligrapher Tsan Hsiang	
1107	Chinese Emperor Hui Tsung writes *A General View of Tea* in which a first mention of the tea whisk is made	Eisai (1141–1215) Myō-e (1173–1232)
1191	Eisai returns from China and plants tea in Hakata, northern Kyushu	
1192	Beginning of the Kamakura period (1192–1333), seat of government moved to Kamakura	
1207	Myō-e is given tea seeds by Eisai and plants them in Togano-o, Kyoto	
1211	Eisai writes *Kissa Yōjōki* or *Tea-drinking is Good for Health*	
1214	Eisai presents his book to the shogun Sanetomo and recommends powdered tea to him	
1215	Eisai dies at the age of 75	
1221	Myō-e transfers his tea bushes from Togano-o to Uji, which is now the largest tea producing area in Japan	
1227	The first tea caddy is brought by Dōgen, a priest, from China	
1228	The first Seto kiln is built by Katō Tōshirōzaemon Kagemasa, who studied potting in China	
1239	The priest Eison holds a large tea gathering at Saidai-ji	

1267	Nampo Jōmyō brings back books on tea and a stand (*daisu*) from China, which were later inherited by Musō Soseki
1274	The Mongols attack northern Kyushu
1278	Fall of the Sung dynasty of China
1280	Mongols succeed in conquering China and the Yuan dynasty (1280–1368) is established
1281	Chinese troops attack Hakata, northern Kyushu
1324	Emperor Godaigo's retainer holds a tea gathering
1332	*Tōcha* gatherings gain popularity
1333	Fall of the Kamakura government and civil war between the Northern and Southern dynasties begins
1336	Ashikaga Takauji, founder of the Ashikaga shougunate, forbids tea gatherings and passes a new law, *Kemmu Shikimoku*
1339	Musō Soseki founds Tenryū-ji
1343	*Tōcha* gatherings regain popularity after the ban
1361	Sasaki Dōyo makes rules for the decoration of the *shoin* tea room
1368	Fall of the Yuan dynasty and start of the Ming dynasty (1368–1644) of China
1392	Southern and Northern dynasties united after sixty years of war and the Muromachi period (1393–1573) is established
1397	The Kinkaku-ji (Golden Pavilion) and thirteen other buildings constructed by Ashikaga Yoshimitsu in Kitayama, Kyoto
1403	Tea is sold by the cup
1417	Retainers of Prince Fushimi hold a tea gathering
1467	Civil war resumes and the Daitoku-ji is burnt down
1470	A *rinkan* tea ceremony is held by Sumitane
1476	*Kundaikan Sōchō-ki* written by Sōami for Ashikaga Yoshimasa containing drawings and descriptions of tea utensils and ink paintings
1482	The Ginkaku-ji (Silver Pavilion) is constructed by Ashikaga Yoshimasa at Higashiyama, Kyoto
1490	Death of Ashikaga Yoshimasa
1502	Death of Murata Shukō
1533	Matsuya Hisamasa starts the *Record of Tea Gatherings*
1540	Rikyū becomes a pupil of Takeno Jō-ō
1548	Sōtatsu starts *Diary of Tea Gatherings*
1549	St. Francisco Xavier comes to Japan
1555	Sōgyū records all the tea gatherings to which he was invited, an account he continues until 1587. Takeno Jō-ō dies
1566	Sōgyū records his own tea ceremonies, an account he continues until 1585

Murata Shukō (1422–1502)
Furuichi Harima (1459–1508)

Takeno Jō-ō (1502–55)
Tsuda Sōtatsu (1504–66)
Tsuda Sōgyū (?–1591)
Imai Sōkyū (1520–93)
Sen no Rikyū (1522–91)
Oda Nobunaga (1534–82)
Toyotomi Hideyoshi (1536–98)
Shimai Sōshitsu (1539–1615)
Sen no Dō-an (1546–1607)

1573	Defeat of the Ashikagas by Oda Nobunaga brings about the end of the Muromachi period and the beginning of the Azuchi period	Sen no Shōan (1546–1614)
1582	Nobunaga is forced to commit suicide by Akechi Mitsuhide, who is in turn defeated in a battle by Toyotomi Hideyoshi. Beginning of the Momoyama period. Rikyū meets Hideyoshi for the first time at a tea gathering held at Himeji Castle	Tokugawa Ieyasu (1542–1616) Yamanoue Sōji (1544–90) Furuta Oribe (1544–1615) Oda Uraku (1547–1621) Matsuya Hisamasa (1551–98) Matsuya Hisayoshi (1598–?)
1583	Rikyū becomes Hideyoshi's *sadō*	Kamiya Sōtan (1551–1635)
1585	Hideyoshi promoted to chief advisor to the emperor and holds a tea ceremony at a small palace inside the Imperial Palace. Rikyū receives the title *Koji*	Honami Kōetsu (1558–1637) Hosokawa Sansai (1563–1645) Konoe Nobutada (1565–1614)
1586	Hideyoshi performs a tea ceremony at the Imperial Palace using his portable gold tea pavilion	Sen no Sōtan (1578–1658) Kobori Enshū (1579–1647)
1587	Hideyoshi's palatial home, the Jurakudai, is built in Kyoto. The "Great Tea Ceremony" of Kitano is held, where Rikyū, Sōgyū and Sōkyū acted as *sadō*	Kanamori Sōwa (1584–1656) Shōkadō Shōjō (1584–1639)
1588	Yamanoue Sōji writes *Book of Famous Tea Utensils*	
1589	*Record of Yamanoue Sōji* completed	
1590	Death of Yamanoue Sōji	
1591	Rikyū commits suicide at the age of 71	
1592	Invasion of Korea	
1593	Death of Imai Sōkyū	
1597	Second invasion of Korea	
1598	Hideyoshi holds a cherry-blosson-viewing ceremony in Kyoto. Death of Hideyoshi at the age of 63	
1600	Battle of Sekigahara and end of the Momoyama period	
1601	Dō-an becomes *sadō* to Hosokawa Sansai	
1603	Edo period (1603–1867) founded by Tokugawa Ieyasu in Edo, present-day Tokyo	
1605	Kobori Enshū constructs the Kohō-an in the Daitoku-ji	Katagiri Sekishū (1605–73)
1607	Dō-an dies at the age of 62	
1610	Furuta Oribe goes to Edo to serve the second Tokugawa shogun	Fujimura Yōken (1613–99)
1614	Battle between the Tokugawas and the Toyotomis. Death of Sen no Shōan at the age of 69, and of Konoe Nobutada at the age of 50	
1615	Another battle between the Tokugawas and the Toyotomis in which the latter were defeated. Suicide of Oribe at the age of 72	
1616	White porcelain produced for the first time by Kanagae Sambei. Death of Tokugawa Ieyasu aged 75	
1618	Jo-an constructed in the Kennin-ji by Oda Uraku	
1620	The first tea ceremony held at Edo Castle accompanied by a of gun salute	
1625	The Katsura Imperial Villa completed	Yamada Sohen (1627–1708) Sugiki Fusai (1628–1706)
1637	Death of Kōetsu at the age of 81	Kusumi Soan (1634–1727)

1641	Hosokawa Sansai writes *Book of Tea*
1644	Fall of the Ming dynasty of China
1645	Hosokawa Sansai dies at the age of 82
1647	Sen no Sōtan retires from the world; death of Enshū
1654	The Chinese priest Ingen (Yin-yuan) comes to Japan and introduces the ceremony using leaf tea
1658	Sōtan dies at the age of 81
1659	The Shūgaku-in Imperial Villa completed
1665	Katagiri Sekishū becomes teacher of tea to the Tokugawas
1690	Yamada Sōhen writes *Sadō Benmō Shō*, and the teachings of Rikyū are discovered in the seven-volume *Nanbō-roku*
1700	Kusumi Soan writes *Chawa Shigetsu Shū*
1706	Death of Sugiki Fusai at the age of 79
1707	Death of Yamada Sōhen
1724	Yamashina Dōan writes about tea ceremonies which he attended which is titled *Kaiki*
1787	Matsudaira Fumai writes *Kokon Meibutsu Ruijū* in which he records all the famed tea utensils in existence
1793	The Kohō-an is burnt down
1811	Matsudaira Fumai writes about the origins of Seto ware in *Seto-tōki Ranshō*
1847	*Sadō Sentei* published by Kawakami Fuhaku who records Joshinsai's teachings
1859	Ii Naosuke completes his work on the tea ceremony called *Cha-no-yu Ichie-shū*
1860	Ii Naosuke is killed outside the gate to Edo Castle
1868	Beginning of the Meiji period (1868–1912)
1898	Dai Nippon Chadō Gakkai founded by Tanaka Senshō
1905	Tanaka Senshō publishes *Chazen Ichimi*
1906	*The Book of Tea* published by Okakura Kakuzo in New York
1913	Death of Okakura Kakuzo

Yabunouchi Chikushin
(1678–1745)

Kawakami Fuhaku (1716–1807)
Hayami Sōtatsu (1740–1809)
Matsudaira Fumai (1751–1818)

Ii Naosuke (1815–60)

Okakura Kakuzo (1862–1913)

PLAN OF TEA ROOMS

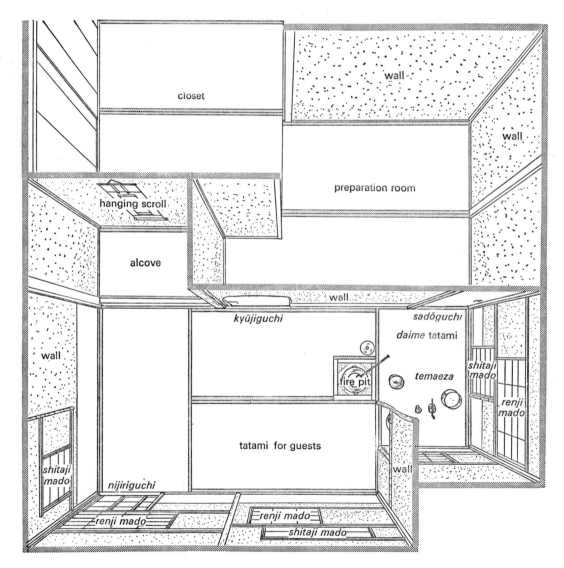

closet

wall

wall

hanging scroll

preparation room

alcove

wall

kyūjiguchi

sadōguchi

daime tatami

wall

fire pit

temaeza

shitaji mado

renji mado

tatami for guests

wall

shitaji mado

nijiriguchi

renji mado

renji mado

shitaji mado

THREE-MAT *DAIME* TATAMI ROOM

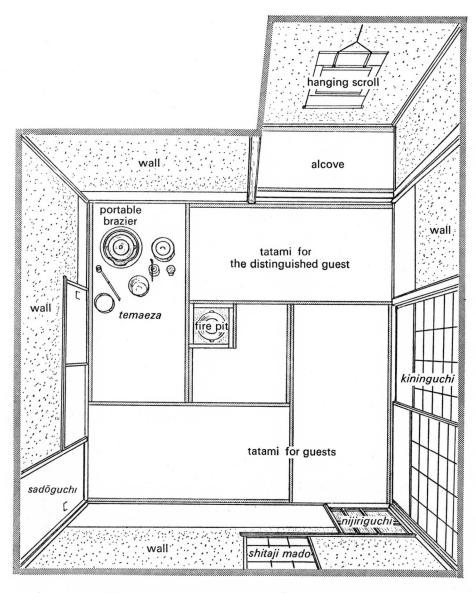

hanging scroll

wall

alcove

portable
brazier

wall

tatami for
the distinguished guest

wall

temaeza

fire pit

kininguchi

tatami for guests

sadōguchi

nijiriguchi

wall

shitaji mado

FOUR-AND-A-HALF-MAT *SŌAN* TEA ROOM